baby BEASTIES

MONSTER MITTENS, HATS & OTHER KNITS
FOR BABIES & TODDLERS

Debby Ware

The Taunton Press

The Taunton Press
Inspiration for hands-on living®

The Taunton Press, Inc., 63 South Main Street
PO Box 5506, Newtown, CT 06470-5506
e-mail: tp@taunton.com

Editors: Ashley Little, Shawna Mullen, Tim Stobierski
Copy Editor: Betty Christiansen
Indexer: Barbara Mortenson
Art Director: Rosalind Loeb Wanke
Cover & Interior Design: Kimberly Adis
Layout: Kimberly Adis
Illustrator: Christine Erikson
Photographer: Alexandra Grablewski
Prop & Wardrobe Stylist: Kimberly Fields

The following names/manufacturers appearing in *Baby Beasties*
are trademarks: Lion Brand®, LB Collection® Superwash Merino,
MinnowMerino™, Plymouth Yarn®, Styrofoam®

A catalog record for this book is available from the United States Library
of Congress.
ISBN # 978-1-63186-004-1

Printed in the United States of America
10 9 8 7 6 5 4 3 2 1

babyBEASTIES

DEDICATION

For my son, Owen, who, even as an adult, has never allowed me to create and knit a single hat, sweater, or scarf for him. I still love him dearly, and he continues to be the best of everything in my life.

ACKNOWLEDGMENTS

I design all my work on my needles in a very small and quiet space. I show my work to a very few select members of my family for their opinion about a finished pattern, and I can always count on their continued encouraging responses. Then off these hard-worked patterns go to my editor at Taunton Press, Shawna Mullen, whom, again, I can count on for her enthusiastic response. Thank you to my family and to Shawna for constantly being my barometer and helping me continue to create.

CONTENTS

WATER

AIR

APPENDIX

INTRODUCTION

KNITTING HAS ENRICHED MY LIFE AND HAS BECOME ONE OF MY FAVORITE ways to express my creativity. Knitting for babies is my passion and, through the years, I have enjoyed creating hats, sweaters, booties, and mittens that are not your typical knitted baby patterns. Unique and unusual are my guiding lights!

If I am sitting, I am knitting, and these small projects are perfect if you are traveling or want to create something fun and fast and useful. From a wide-mouthed lion looking up into the sky, to a giant clawed crab, to a fanciful flying pig, these patterns are meant to bring fun and warmth to anyone who wears them (and a laugh or two to anyone seeing them worn on a little one).

I design my patterns on my needles, which is a good and bad process. It's good because the idea in my head lets my fingers just fly trying to produce whatever it is I have dreamt up. It's bad because I end up with quite a few bad starts (and finishes). It is a process that I have become accustomed to, but one that also leaves me with many failures in a basket, waiting to be unraveled and knitted into something else. But you don't need to be afraid to create the beasts in this book—I've selected only the best of the best finished projects to share with you here. Carefully written, step-by-step, clear instructions will ensure that you have no frustrations. There will be no failures in your basket!

I have chosen yarns that are readily available, easy to care for, and lovely to knit with. Also, my thrifty side kicks in! Where only a small amount of one color is called for in one pattern, I tried to use that same yarn and color in a larger quantity in another pattern so that you don't need to worry about waste.

There is always something very special about knitting for babies and children, and I hope you will find the beasts in this book easy to create for all the little ones in your world.

LAND

clucking
CHICKEN CAP

This chicken will sit on your little chick's head,
keeping his head warm just like she
keeps her eggs warm!

SIZING

One Size: 18-in. to 20-in. circumference

YARN

DK weight/light worsted weight yarn
The cap shown is made with Plymouth Yarn®
    DK Merino Superwash: 100% fine superwash
    merino wool, 1.75 oz. (50 g)/130 yd. (119 m)

YARDAGE

80 yd. Merino Superwash #1117 Light Grey
25 yd. DK Merino Superwash #1123 Peapod
2 yd. DK Merino Superwash #1126 Tangerine
5 yd. DK Merino Superwash #1118 Dark Grey
15 yd. DK Merino Superwash #1020 Butter
2 yd. DK Merino Superwash #1108 Sunshine

MATERIALS

16-in. U.S. size 5 circular needle
Four U.S. size 5 double-pointed needles
Stitch marker
Tapestry needle

GAUGE

5½ sts = 1 in.

DIRECTIONS FOR CAP

HAT BASE

With circ needle and Peapod, CO 100 sts. Place
    a st marker on right needle and, beginning
    Rnd 1, join CO sts together making sure
    that sts do not become twisted on needle.
    P1 rnd.
K all rnds until piece measures 2 in.
Cut Peapod and attach Light Grey. K all rnds
    until entire piece measures 7 in.

TAIL

At beginning of round, K12 sts. Turn work.
P2tog and P11 sts. Turn work.
K9 sts, K2tog. Turn work.
Continue in established pattern, decreasing
    at established end, until 3 sts remain.
    BO all sts.
Attach yarn on opposite side and repeat for
    second side of tail, reversing decrease end.

BODY MIDDLE SEAM

Attach Light Grey at the bottom of the tail with RS facing and BO 25 sts. Work center 26 sts (for head) and BO remaining 25 sts.

HEAD

Place remaining sts on 3 dpns. With Butter and working in the round, beginning at the seam, work 12 rnds.

Dec Rnd:*K4, K2tog; rep from * to last 2 sts, K2.
K2 rnds.
BO all sts.

BEAK

With Tangerine and 2 dpns, create a 6-st I-Cord (p. 114). Work 4 rows. K2tog, K2, K2tog. K3 rows. BO all sts.

FINISHING

With Light Grey, sew body middle seam closed from tip of tail to back of chicken's head. With Tangerine, create a 3-st I-cord long enough to fit around the top of the chicken's head. BO all sts. Using a small running st, attach to top of chicken head, closing the opening as you sew. Attach beak to front of chicken's head. Using Dark Grey and Duplicate Stitch (p. 113), create a circular pattern for chicken's wings.

knitting tip

The general pattern for this project can be adapted to create many other types of birds by simply adjusting the colors of yarn used.

Using Butter and a small running st, create an oval/circular pattern around chicken's breast.

Using Sunshine and Duplicate Stitch, decorate middle of breast so that it has feathers.

Using Dark Grey, create 2 French Knots (p. 113) for chicken's eyes.

Monstrosity
MITTENS AND HAT

With a wide, toothy smile and a whole lot of wild hair and spikes, this friendly monster peeks out from the top of this hat while the two smaller beasts help battle beastly cold hands.

Monstrosity Mittens

SIZING

Small (1–2 years)
Large (2–4 years)
Figures for larger size are given below in parentheses. Where only one set of figures appears, the directions apply to both sizes.

YARN

Worsted weight, single-ply yarn
The mittens shown on p. 12 are made with Classic Elite MinnowMerino™: 100% extra-fine superwash merino, 1.75 oz. (50 g)/77 yd. (70 m).

YARDAGE

50 (60) yd. MinnowMerino #4735 Chartreuse
30 (40) yd. MinnowMerino #4755 Cerise
8 yd. MinnowMerino #4750 Goldie
Small amounts of fingering or DK weight white scrap yarn
Small amounts of fingering or DK weight black scrap yarn

MATERIALS

16-in. U.S. size 8 circular needle
Two U.S. size 8 double-pointed needles
Tapestry needle
Stitch markers
Stitch holders

GAUGE

18 sts = 4 in.

DIRECTIONS FOR MITTENS

CUFF

With circ needle and Chartreuse, CO 27 (31) sts. Working back and forth on circ needle, work in K2, P2 ribbing for 1¼ (2) in.
Work in St st for 2 rows.
NEXT ROW (INC): K12 (14) sts, place marker, K1f&b, K1, K1f&b, place marker, K12 (14).
P1 row.
NEXT ROW (INC): K12 (14) sts, sl marker, K1f&b, K3, K1f&b, sl marker, K12 (14).
P1 row.

knitting tip

Cut tails long after binding off each color. It's easier to sew up the mittens with those matching yarns.

NEXT ROW (INC): K12 (14) sts, sl marker, K1f&b, K5, K1f&b, sl marker, K12 (14).

P1 row.

NEXT ROW (INC): K12 (14), sl marker, K1f&b, K7, K1f&b, sl marker, K12 (14).

P1 row.

SIZE LARGE ONLY

NEXT ROW (INC): K14, sl marker, K1f&b, K9, K1f&b, sl marker, K14.

BOTH SIZES

DIVIDING ROW (RS): K to marker and place these worked sts on a holder. Remove marker, K9 (11) for thumb, remove second marker, place remaining 12 (14) sts on st holder.

THUMB

Turn work.

P thumb sts.

Turn work. Continue in St st on the 9 (11) thumb sts until thumb measures 1 (1½) in. from cast-on edge, ending after a P (WS) row.

ROW 1 (DEC): *K1, K2tog; rep from * across entire row.

ROW 2: P.

ROW 3 (DEC): *K2tog; rep from * across row.

Cut yarn, leaving a 2-in. tail. Thread a tapestry needle and draw end through remaining sts. Pull tightly through all sts. Fasten securely.

BODY

Sl sts from first holder to needle and join yarn.

K12 (14), sl sts from second holder onto the same needle, K12 (14).

P1 row.

HAIR

Drop Chartreuse and attach Cerise.

ROW 1: Work Loop Stitch (see p. 114) across row.

ROW 2: K.

ROW 3: Work Loop Stitch across row.

ROW 4: K.

FACE AND NOSE

Cut Cerise and pick up Chartreuse.

Work even in St st until entire piece measures 3½ (4½) in. from top of ribbing cuff, ending with a P row.

ROW 1 (DEC): *K2, K2tog; rep from * across row.

ROW 2: P.

ROW 3 (DEC): *K1, K2tog; rep from * across row.

ROW 4: P.

ROW 5 (DEC): K2tog across entire row.

Cut yarn, leaving an 8-in. tail. Thread a tapestry needle and draw through all sts on needle. Pull tightly and secure on WS of work.

FINISHING

NOTE: When you knit the second mitten, make sure thumbs are facing in opposite directions before creating eyes and mouth so that both of these Monstrosity Mittens are face side up.

With Chartreuse and tapestry needle, sew thumb seam and side seam of mitten.

Weave in all loose ends.

With Goldie and dpns, create 6 I-Cords (see p. 114) as follows: CO 3 sts. Create an I-Cord 1½ in. long. Cut yarn, leaving a 3-in. tail. Thread tapestry needle and pass through sts on needle. Work needle through the entire cord until you have both the CO tail and the working tail on the same end of the cord. Attach I-Cords around the entire mitten under the first row of Loop Stitches.

With black scrap yarn and a tapestry needle, create 2 French Knots (see p. 113) for eyes. With Cerise and a tapestry needle, sew a running st to create a smile or smirk. With white scrap yarn and tapestry needle, sew small vertical sts across smile to give the monster some teeth!

Monstrosity Hat

SIZING

Small (15-in. circumference)

Large (19-in. circumference)

Figures for larger size are given below in
parentheses. Where only one set of
figures appears, the directions apply
to both sizes.

YARN

Worsted weight, single-ply yarn

The hat shown is made with Classic Elite
MinnowMerino: 100% extra-fine superwash
merino, 1.75 oz. (50 g)/77 yd. (70 m).

YARDAGE

50 (70) yd. MinnowMerino #4735 Chartreuse

30 (40) yd. MinnowMerino #4755 Cerise

8 yd. MinnowMerino #4750 Goldie

Small amounts of fingering or DK weight white
scrap yarn

Small amount of DK weight black scrap yarn
for eyes

MATERIALS

16-in. U.S. size 8 circular needle

Two U.S. size 8 double-pointed needles

Tapestry needle

Stitch marker

GAUGE

18 sts = 4 in.

FINGERS

Using Cable Cast-On (see p. 112), CO 6 sts.
Immediately BO all 6 sts.

DIRECTIONS FOR HAT

HAT BASE

With Chartreuse and circ needle,
CO 60 (70) sts.
P1 rnd.
Work K1, P1 ribbing for 5 rnds.
K1 rnd.

FINGERS

Drop Chartreuse and attach Cerise.
FINGER RND: *With Cerise, create 1 finger.
Drop Cerise and K4 with Chartreuse;
rep from * for entire rnd.
Cut Cerise and, with Chartreuse, K6 rnds.
NEXT RND (DEC): *K8, K2tog; rep from *
for entire rnd.
K3 rnds.
NEXT RND (DEC): *K7, K2tog; rep from *
for entire rnd.
K3 rnds.
Continue in established dec rnds until you have
completed K4, K2tog rnd.

WILD HAIR

Drop Chartreuse and attach Cerise.
With Cerise, work first Loop Stitch
(see p. 114) rnd.

K1 rnd.
Work second Loop Stitch rnd.
Cut Cerise and pick up Chartreuse.
K1 rnd.
NEXT RND (DEC): *K3, K2tog; rep from * for
entire rnd.
K2 rnds.
NEXT RND (DEC): *K2, K2tog; rep from * for
entire rnd.
K1 rnd.
NEXT RND (DEC): *K1, K2tog; rep from * for
entire rnd.
K2tog for entire rnd. Cut yarn, leaving a 6-in. tail.
Pass tapestry needle through remaining sts
on needle. Pull yarn tightly and secure to WS
of work.

FINISHING

With Goldie and dpns, create eight 1½-in.-long
I-Cords (see p. 114). Cut yarn, leaving a 3-in.
tail. Thread tapestry needle and pass tail
through sts on needle. Work needle through
the entire cord until you have both the CO
tail and the working tail on the same end
of the cord. Using the tails to seam, attach
each I-Cord in a circle around the crown of
the hat, just beneath the Loop Stitches. With
tapestry needle and Cerise, create a smile
or smirk with a running st. With scraps of
white, and using photograph for placement,
create teeth by making vertical sts on top of
the monster's smile. With black scrap yarn,
create 2 French Knots (see p. 113) for eyes.
Weave in all loose ends.

Wild Thing
OGRE CAP

Wild Thing! You make my heart sing!
This ogre, with its enormous face and smile, will scare the cold away and keep your little one cozy.

SIZING

Small (16-in. circumference)
Large (18-in. circumference)
Figures for larger size are given below in parentheses. Where only one set of figures appears, the directions apply to both sizes.

YARN

DK weight/light worsted weight yarn
The cap shown is made with Lion Brand® LB Collection® Superwash Merino: 100% superwash merino wool, 3.5 oz. (100 g)/306 yd. (280 m).

YARDAGE

60 (80) yd. Superwash Merino #127 Mahogany
50 yd. Superwash Merino #170 Dijon
30 yd. Superwash Merino #098 Ivory
20 yd. Superwash Merino #114 Cayenne
15 yd. Superwash Merino #153 Night Sky
5 yd. fingering or DK weight yellow scrap yarn for eyes

MATERIALS

16-in. U.S. size 5 circular needle
Four U.S. size 5 double-pointed needles
One pair U.S. size 5 straight needles
Stitch marker
Tapestry needle
Crochet hook
Small amount of polyester filling (optional)

GAUGE

24 sts = 4 in.

DIRECTIONS FOR CAP

CAP BASE

With circ needle and Mahogany, CO 100 (120) sts. Place a st marker on right needle and, beginning Rnd 1, join CO sts together making sure that sts do not become twisted on needle.
P1 rnd.
Drop Mahogany and attach Dijon.
RIDGE RND 1: *K1, sl 1 wyib; rep from * to end of rnd.
RIDGE RND 2: *P1, sl 1 wyib; rep from * to end of rnd.
Drop Dijon and pick up Mahogany.
RIDGE RND 3: K.

RIDGE RND 4: P.

Rep these 4 rnds twice.

Cut Dijon and pick up Mahogany.

K all rnds until entire piece measures 7 (9) in.

DEC RND: K2tog for entire rnd.

Rep Dec Rnd, placing sts on dpns when necessary, until approx 6–8 sts remain. Cut yarn, leaving a 6-in. tail. Thread a tapestry needle and pass through remaining sts.

FACE

With Dijon and straight needles, CO 25 sts.

ROW 1 (INC): K1f&b, K to last st, K1f&b.

ROW 2: P.

Rep these 2 rows until there are 35 sts.

Work 10 rows in St st.

NEXT ROW (DEC): Ssk, K to last 2 sts, K2tog.

NEXT ROW: P.

Rep these 2 rows until there are 25 sts.

BO all sts.

With tapestry needle and Dijon, sew this base to the front of the cap, placing the bottom edge of the base at the top of ridge sts.

★ knitting tip

Don't have a crochet hook on hand? Use a tapestry needle to pull the strands of hair through each stitch.

LARGE HEAD HORNS

(MAKE 2)

With Ivory and straight needles, CO 12 sts.

ROWS 1–4: Work even in St st.

ROW 5 (DEC): SSK, K to last 2 sts, K2tog.

ROWS 6–8: Work even in St st.

ROW 9: Rep Row 5.

ROWS 10–12: Work even in St st.

ROW 13: (K2tog) across the entire row.

ROW 14: P.

BO.

Fold each horn in half lengthwise with WS together. Sew the long seam of the horns. If desired, place a small amount of polyester filling into each horn to help it stand up straight. With tapestry needle and Ivory, attach horns to the top sides of face base.

EYES

With yellow scrap yarn and straight needles, CO 6 sts.

Working in Seed st, work approx 6 rows or until you have created a square. Cut yarn, leaving a 6-in. tail. Thread a tapestry needle and pass it through the sts on the needle, then sew a running st along the other 3 sides of the square. Pull tightly until you have created a ball. Secure all loose ends.

Thread a tapestry needle with Night Sky and create a French Knot (see p. 113) in the middle of each eye.

SMALL HORN EYEBROWS AND NOSE HORN

(MAKE 3)

With Cayenne and straight needles, CO 12 sts. K1 row.

Beginning with a P (WS) row and working in St st, P2tog at each end of the next and every foll row until 2 sts remain.

NEXT ROW: K2tog.

BO. Cut yarn, leaving a 6-in. tail.

FINISHING

With tapestry needle and Ivory, create French Knots around each eyebrow. With tapestry needle and Cayenne, sew the long seam of the horn and attach to cap above eyes.

With tapestry needle and yarn tails, sew nose horn to center of face.

Thread a tapestry needle with Night Sky and create a smirky smile across the face using a small running st.

Thread a tapestry needle with Ivory and create small French Knots along the base of the smirk you just created for a toothy grin!

For hair, cut approx thirty-five 8-in. strands of Night Sky. Hold one strand of yarn and fold it in half. Using a crochet hook, insert the hook under a st near the ears, hook the strand of folded yarn in the middle, and pull partway through the st. Pass the yarn ends through the loop formed and pull to secure. Continue with this method around large head horns and side of the Wild Thing's face. Snip to different lengths for that raggedy and wild look!

Somewhat Silly
SERPENT SCARF
WITH WILD WART NOSE

Here is a great solution for lost mittens: Tuck the mittens into each end of the scarf. Kids will never have to wonder where their mittens went!

SIZING
One size

YARN
Worsted weight, single-ply yarn
The scarf shown is made with Classic Elite MinnowMerino: 100% extra-fine superwash merino, 1.75 oz. (50 g)/77 yd. (70 m).

YARDAGE
140 yd. MinnowMerino #4797 Olive
120 yd. MinnowMerino #4785 Orangini
60 yd. MinnowMerino #4755 Cerise
30 yd. MinnowMerino #4750 Goldie
2 yd. MinnowMerino #4716 Lamb's White

MATERIALS
One pair plus one extra U.S. size 8 straight needles
Two U.S. size 8 double-pointed needles
Tapestry needle
Stitch marker
Stitch holder
Small amount of polyester filling (optional)

GAUGE
18 sts = 4 in.

SEED STITCH
Row 1: *K1, P1; rep from * to end of row.
All other rows: K the P sts and P the K sts.

DIRECTIONS FOR SCARF

MITTEN BODY
(MAKE 2)
**With straight needles and Orangini, CO 13 sts.
K1 row. P1 row.
ROW 3 (INC): K to last st, K1f&b.
ROW 4: P.
Rep Rows 3 and 4 until there are 19 sts on needle.
NEXT ROW (DEC): SSK, K to last 2 sts, K2tog.
Rep this row until 11 sts remain, ending after a WS row.
Work 4 rows in St st.
NEXT ROW (INC): K1f&b, K to last st, K1f&b.
Rep this row every 4th row (RS) until there are 21 sts on needle.
Cut Orangini. Place all sts on st holder.

With Cerise, create a second identical piece, but leave sts on needle when complete. Cut Cerise.

Transfer Orangini sts from holder onto needle, making sure both Orangini and Cerise sts are on the needle with RS facing.

Attach Olive.

Work 16 rows in St st.

RIBBING ROW: Work K1, P1 ribbing for 21 sts, place marker, work K1, P1 ribbing to end of row.

NEXT ROW: Work Seed st for 21 sts, sl marker, work ribbing to end of row.

Continue in established ribbing and Seed st pattern for 1 in., ending with RS facing.

BO 21 ribbing sts. Remove marker and continue in Seed st until piece measures 12 in. from top of mitten ribbing.

Cut Olive and attach Orangini.

Continue in Seed st until piece measures 18 in. from top of mitten ribbing.

Place sts on holder.

Rep from ** to create a second piece. Leave sts on needle.

Transfer sts from st holder onto a second needle. BO all sts using Three-Needle Bind-Off (see p. 114).

WILD WART NOSE (MAKE 2)

With straight needles and Cerise, CO 12 sts.

K1 row. P1 row.

Beginning with a K (RS) row and working in St st, K2tog at each end of the next and every following row until 2 sts remain.

NEXT ROW: K2tog.

BO. Cut yarn, leaving a 4-in. tail.

EYEBROW
(MAKE 4)

With dpns and Goldie, CO 3. Create an I-Cord (see p. 113) 6 in. long. Cut yarn, leaving a 4-in. tail. Thread a tapestry needle and pass through sts on the needle, then pass the needle through the center of the I-Cord to bring both tails to the same end. Pull tightly to create a squiggle.

TONGUE
(MAKE 2)

With straight needles and Orangini, CO 6 sts.
Work in St st for 6 rows.
BO all sts. Cut yarn, leaving a 6-in. tail.

FINISHING

Thread a tapestry needle with Goldie and, using Duplicate Stitch (see p. 113), stitch giant circles centered at top of Orangini work for eyes. With tapestry needle and Lamb's White, sew a running st around each circle. With tapestry needle and Cerise, create 2 French Knots (see p. 113) in center of each Goldie circle.

Thread a tapestry needle with Goldie and create warts on the serpent's nose with randomly placed French Knots. Sew the long seam of the nose and stuff lightly with polyester filling, if desired.

With tapestry needle and yarn tails, attach nose and eyebrows to mitten. Join side seams of upper and lower jaw, leaving back of mouth open. Sew side seams to attach ribbed mitten edge to scarf. Sew tongue to inside of mouth and sew back of mouth closed.

knitting tip

You have the option of using either a straight needle or a dpn for the Three-Needle Bind-Off.

Abominable
SNOWMAN
CAP AND SCARF

A snowman with a cozy cap will be sure to keep your little polar bear warm! Two small snowmen pockets at each end of the scarf double as mittens to help keep your little snowman even warmer.

Abominable Snowman Cap

SIZING

Small (17-in. circumference)
Large (24-in. circumference)
Figures for larger size are given below in parentheses. Where only one set of figures appears, the directions apply to both sizes.

YARN

Worsted weight, single-ply yarn
The cap shown is made with Classic Elite MinnowMerino: 100% extra-fine superwash merino, 1.75 oz. (50 g)/77 yd. (70 m).

YARDAGE

110 (140) yd. MinnowMerino #4701 Snow White
40 yd. MinnowMerino #4758 Rogue
4 yd. MinnowMerino #4785 Orangini
4 yd. MinnowMerino #4713 Jet Black
Small amount of black fingering weight scrap yarn

MATERIALS

16-in. U.S. size 8 circular needle
Four U.S. size 8 double-pointed needles
Stitch marker
Tapestry needle

GAUGE

18 sts = 4 in.

SEED STITCH

RND 1: *K1, P1: rep from * to end of rnd.
ALL OTHER RNDS: K the P sts and P the K sts.

DIRECTIONS FOR CAP

CAP BASE

With circ needle and Snow White, CO 80 (100) sts. Place a st marker on right needle and, beginning Rnd 1, join CO sts together making sure that sts do not become twisted on needle.
P1 rnd.
Work in Seed st for 4 (5) in.

DECREASE ROUNDS

RND 1 (DEC): *K8, K2tog; rep from * to end of rnd.

RNDS 2 AND 3: Work even in Seed st.

RND 4 (DEC): *K7, K2tog; rep from * to end of rnd.

RNDS 5 AND 6: Work even in Seed st.

Continue in established dec pattern, knitting 1 less st between dec and changing to dpns when necessary. Continue until you have finished the K3, K2tog rnd.

Work even on remaining sts for 6 (8) rnds.

NEXT RND: *K2, K2tog; rep from * to end of rnd.

NEXT RND: *K2tog; rep from * to end of rnd.

Cut yarn, leaving a 6-in. tail. Thread yarn tail through tapestry needle and pass through remaining 2–4 sts. Pull tightly and secure on WS.

SNOWMAN CAP

With circ needle and Rogue, CO 80 sts. Place a st marker on right needle and, beginning Rnd 1, join CO sts together making sure that sts do not become twisted on needle.

P1 rnd.

K2 rnds.

NEXT RND (DEC): *K8, K2tog; rep from * to end of rnd.

K2 rnds.

NEXT RND (DEC): *K7, K2tog; rep from * to end of rnd.

K2 rnds.

Continue in dec pattern, knitting 1 st less between decs and continuing to K2 rnds between dec rounds (placing sts on dpns when necessary) until you have finished *K3, K2tog rnd.

Work on remaining sts for 6 (8) rnds.

NEXT RND (DEC): *K2, K2tog; rep from * to end of rnd.

NEXT RND (DEC): *K2tog; rep from * to end of rnd.

With remaining 2–4 sts on needle, create an I-Cord (see p. 114) approx 8 in. long. BO all sts.

CHARCOAL EYES
(MAKE 2)

With Jet Black and circ needle, CO 10 sts. Working back and forth in Seed st, work approx 8 rows or until you have created a square. Cut yarn, leaving a 6-in. tail. Thread a tapestry needle and pass it through the sts on the needle, then sew a running st along the other 3 sides of the square. Pull tightly until you have created a ball. Secure all loose ends.

Rep to create a second eye.

CARROT NOSE

With Orangini and circ needle, CO 10 sts. Working back and forth, P1 row.

Working in St st, dec 1 st at each end every other row until 6 sts remain.

Work 3 rows in St st.

Dec 1 st at each end every other row until you have 2 sts. BO all sts.

FINISHING

With black scrap yarn and tapestry needle, embroider a small smile under the nose. Sew eyes onto snowman's face.

With Orangini and tapestry needle, attach carrot nose to snowman's face.

knitting tip

* You should use either cotton or wool for this hat and scarf set. Metal needles will keep the stitches moving fast, while wooden needles may be better for beginners.

Abominable Snowman Scarf

SIZING
One size

YARN
Worsted weight, single-ply yarn
The scarf shown is made with Classic Elite
    MinnowMerino: 100% extra-fine superwash
    merino, 1.75 oz. (50 g)/77 yd. (70 m).

YARDAGE
140 yd. MinnowMerino #4701 Snow White
4 yd. MinnowMerino #4785 Orangini
4 yd. MinnowMerino #4713 Jet Black
Small amount of black fingering weight
    scrap yarn

MATERIALS
One pair U.S. size 8 straight needles
16-in. U.S. size 8 circular needle
Two U.S. size 8 double-pointed needles
Tapestry needle

GAUGE
18 sts = 4 in.

DOUBLE MOSS STITCH
ROWS 1 AND 2: *K2, P2; rep from * to end of row.
ROWS 3 AND 4: *P2, K2; rep from * to end
    of row.

SEED STITCH
RND 1: *K1, P1; rep from * to end of rnd.
ALL OTHER RNDS: K the P sts and P the K sts.

DIRECTIONS FOR SCARF

SCARF RIBBING

With Snow White and straight needles, CO
   20 sts.
RIBBING ROW: *K3, P1; rep from * to end of row.
Rep Ribbing Row until piece measures 4 in.
Begin working in Double Moss st, continuing
   until entire piece measures 27 in.

SLIT OPENING

NEXT ROW: Work first 4 sts in Double Moss st,
   BO 16 sts, work last 4 sts in Double Moss st.
NEXT ROW: Work first 4 sts in Double Moss st,
   CO 16 sts, work last 4 sts in Double Moss st.
Continue working Double Moss st until entire
   piece measures 34 in.
Rep Ribbing Row for 4 in. BO all sts.

SNOWMAN POCKET

With RS facing and using circ needle and
   Snow White, pick up 20 sts along one side
   of ribbing, pick up 20 sts along bottom of
   ribbing, and pick up 20 sts along other side
   of scarf at ribbing.
Work Seed st on these 60 sts for 3 rows.
BO 20 sts on one side of pocket.
Work Seed st across bottom 20 sts.
BO 20 sts on other side of pocket.
Cut yarn, leaving a 4-in. tail.
Re-attach yarn to RS of remaining bottom
   20 sts.
Continue to work in Seed st on these 20 sts for
   front of pocket until entire pocket measures
   4 in. BO all sts, leaving a long yarn tail for
   seaming.
With long yarn tails, sew up side seams of
   pockets. Weave in all loose ends.
Rep Snowman Pocket instructions on opposite
   end of scarf.

CARROT NOSE
(MAKE 2)

CO 5 sts onto a dpn.
ROWS 1–5: Work I-Cord (see p. 114).
ROW 6: K2tog, K1, K2tog.
Continue with I-Cord on these 3 sts for 3 rows.
   Cut yarn, leaving a 3-in. tail. Thread tapestry
   needle and pass through 3 sts on needle.
   Work needle through the entire cord until
   you have both the CO tail and the working
   tail on the same end of cord. Use these tails
   to attach the carrot nose to the middle of
   the pocket. Rep for opposite end of scarf.

EYES AND SMILE

With Jet Black and tapestry needle, work
   2 large French Knots (see p. 113) for eyes
   of snowman. With fingering-weight black
   scrap yarn, create 7 small French Knots
   for snowman's smile. Rep for opposite
   end of scarf.

knitting tip

I designed a small slit
in the length of this
scarf so you can pull
one end through. It's
an easy way to keep
this scarf in place!

Ferocious
LION
HAT AND MITTENS

This lion is always looking up and ready for any winds that come, keeping the head that is under it safe and warm! Pair it with toasty matching mittens to really scare the cold away.

Ferocious Lion Hat

SIZING
One size (19-in. to 20-in. circumference)

YARN
DK weight/light worsted weight yarn
The yarn shown is Plymouth Yarn DK Merino Superwash: 100% fine superwash merino wool, 1.75 oz. (50 g)/130 yd. (119 m).

YARDAGE
80 yd. DK Merino Superwash #1124 Sand
40 yd. DK Merino Superwash #1021 Pink
30 yd. DK Merino Superwash #1050 Black
30 yd. DK Merino Superwash #1125 Brown Bear
30 yd. DK Merino Superwash #1000 White
5 yd. DK Merino Superwash #1123 Peapod

MATERIALS
16-in. U.S. size 5 circular needle
One pair U.S. size 5 straight needles
Two U.S. size 5 double-pointed needles
Stitch marker
Tapestry needle
Stitch holder
Crochet hook

GAUGE
22 sts = 4 in

DIRECTIONS FOR HAT

HAT BODY
NOTE: Pattern begins at the top of the hat and the back of the lion's mouth. Make 2, placing first piece on a holder until second piece is completed. Both pieces will then be combined onto a circ needle.

***With Pink and straight needles, CO 40 sts.

INC ROW: *K1f&b, K to last st, K1f&b.*

Continue in St st, working Inc Row on every other row until there are 48 sts.

Work 3 rows in St st.

DEC ROW: **K2tog, K to last 2 sts; K2tog.**

Work Dec Row every other row until 20 sts rem.

P1 row.

Cut Pink and attach Black. K1 row. P1 row.

Cut Black and attach Sand. K2 rows.

Rep Inc Row from * to * every other row until there are 48 sts.

Rep Dec Row from ** to ** every other row until 40 sts rem.***

Place these 40 sts on st holder.

Rep from *** to *** to make a second piece. Place all 80 sts on circ needle.

K4 rnds.

INC RND: *K5, K1f&b; rep from * to end of rnd.

Work 4 rnds.

Rep Inc Rnd.

Continue working until the entire piece measures 4½ in. from where you placed sts on circ needle.

BO all sts.

(MAKE 4 LARGE AND 2 SMALL)

With White and straight needles, CO 10 (15) sts.

Work in Garter st for 3 rows.

DEC ROW: SSK, work in Garter st to last 2 sts, K2tog.

Work Dec Row every other row until 4 sts rem.

LAST ROW: SSK, K2tog.

BO all sts.

EARS

(MAKE 2)

With Brown Bear and straight needles, CO 7 sts.

INC ROW: K1f&b, K to end of row, K1f&b.

Continue to work in St st, working Inc Row every other row until there are 17 sts on needle.

Work 5 rows in St st.

RIDGE ROW (WS): K.

DEC ROW: *SSK, K to end of row, K2tog.*

Continue in St st, working Dec Row every other row until 7 sts rem.

BO all sts.

NOSE

With Black and straight needles, CO 15 sts. Work 2 rows in Seed st.

DEC ROW: SSK, work in Seed st to last 2 sts, K2tog.

Continue in Seed st, working Dec Row every other row until 7 sts rem.

BO all sts.

FINISHING

With tapestry needle and Pink, create small running sts to sew the inside Pink mouth to the outside Sand of the lion's head. Sew the mouth seam closed in the center where the 2 Pink pieces meet. Sew sides of mouth closed to create a 1-in.-long seam.

With Black and dpns, CO 2 sts. Create an I-Cord (see p. 114) long enough to line the lion's mouth opening. With Black and tapestry needle, sew I-Cords to each side of the mouth, looping the 1-in. seam to the inside of the mouth.

Fold each tooth in half. With tapestry needle and White, sew seam of each tooth from point to base to create a small cylinder shape. Sew 2 large teeth to top front of mouth. Sew 2 large teeth to bottom of mouth. Sew the 2 small teeth to each side of the bottom of mouth.

With Black and dpns, CO 2 sts for nose. Create an I-Cord 1 in. long. Sew on to center top lip of lion.

With tapestry needle and Black, sew nose to center top of lion's head.

With tapestry needle and Peapod, and using Duplicate Stitch (see p. 113) and photograph for placement, create 2 circles for eyes. With tapestry needle and Black, outline the Peapod circles with a running stitch.

With tapestry needle and Black, create a French Knot (see p. 113) in the center of the Peapod circle.

Fold lion's ear at Ridge Row with WS together to create a 2-sided ear. Sew seams closed and sew ear to top of head using photograph for placement. Rep for opposite ear.

Cut 20–25 pieces of Sand and 20–25 pieces of Brown Bear each approx 8 in. to 10 in. long for lion's mane. Hold one strand of yarn and fold strand in half. Using a crochet hook, insert the hook under a st near the ears, hook the

strand of folded yarn in the middle, and pull partway through the st. Pass the yarn ends through the loop formed and pull to secure.

Continue around the base of the ears and around the entire hat base, evenly spacing the mane and alternating the 2 colors.

Now let this lion roar the cold away!

Ferocious Lion Mittens

SIZING

One size (7 in. from ribbing to tip of lion's nose)

YARN

DK weight/light worsted weight yarn
The mittens shown are made with Plymouth
   Yarn DK Merino Superwash: 100% fine
   superwash merino wool, 1.75 oz. (50 g)/
   130 yd. (119 m).

YARDAGE

100 yd. DK Merino Superwash #1020 Butter
50 yd. DK Merino Superwash #1021 Pink
30 yd. DK Merino Superwash #1050 Black
30 yd. DK Merino Superwash #1000 White
20 yd. DK Merino Superwash #1125 Brown Bear
10 yd. DK Merino Superwash #1123 Peapod

MATERIALS

One pair U.S. size 5 straight needles
Four U.S. size 5 double-pointed needles

Stitch marker
Tapestry needle
Stitch holder

GAUGE

22 sts = 4 in.

DIRECTIONS FOR MITTENS

MITTEN BODY

NOTE: Pattern begins at the top of the mittens
   and the back of the lion's mouth. Make 2,
   placing first piece on a holder until second
   piece is completed. Both pieces will then be
   combined onto dpns.

***With Pink and straight needles, CO 20 sts.

P1 row.

K1 row.

P1 row.

INC ROW: *K1f&b, K to last st, K1f&b.*

Continue in St st, working Inc Row on every
   other row until there are 30 sts.

DEC ROW: **K2tog, K to last 2 sts, K2tog.**

Work Dec Row every other row until 20 sts rem.

Cut Pink and attach Butter.

Rep Inc Row from * to * every other row until
   there are 30 sts.

Rep Dec Row from ** to ** until 20 sts rem.***

Place these 20 sts on st holder.

Rep from *** to *** to make a second piece.
   Place all 40 sts on 3 dpns.

Cut Pink and attach Butter.

K all rnds until piece measures 4 in. from where
   you placed sts on dpns.

BO all sts.

EARS

(MAKE 2)

With Brown Bear and straight needles, CO 5 sts.

INC ROW: K1f&b, K to end of row, K1f&b.

Continue to work in St st, working Inc Row every other row until there are 11 sts.

RIDGE ROW (WS): K.

DEC ROW: SSK, K to end of row, K2tog.

Continue in St st, working Dec Row every other row until 5 sts remain.

BO all sts.

TEETH

(MAKE 4)

With White and straight needles, CO 10 sts.

Work in Garter st for 3 rows.

DEC ROW: SSK, work in Garter st to last 2 sts, K2tog.

Work Dec Row every other row until 4 sts remain.

LAST ROW: SSK, K2tog.

BO all sts.

NOSE

With Black and straight needles, CO 10 sts. Work 2 rows in Seed st.

DEC ROW: SSK, work in Seed st to last 2 sts, K2tog.

Continue to work in Seed st, working Dec Row every other row until 6 sts remain.

BO all sts.

FINISHING

With tapestry needle and Pink, create small running sts to sew the inside Pink mouth to the outside Sand of the lion's head. Sew the mouth seam closed in the center where the 2 Pink pieces meet. Sew sides of mouth closed to create a 1-in.-long seam.

With Black and dpns, CO 2 sts. Create an I-Cord (see p. 114) long enough to line the lion's mouth opening. With Black and tapestry needle, sew I-Cords to each side of mouth, looping the 1-in. seam to inside of the mouth.

Fold each tooth in half. With tapestry needle and White, sew seam of each tooth from point to base to create a small cylinder shape. Sew 2 teeth to top front of mouth. Sew 2 teeth to bottom of mouth.

With Black and dpns, CO 2 sts for nose. Create an I-Cord 1 in. long. With tapestry needle, sew I-Cord onto center top lip of lion.

With tapestry needle and Black, sew nose to center top of lion's head.

With tapestry needle and Peapod, and using Duplicate Stitch (see p. 113) and photograph for placement, create 2 circles for eyes. With tapestry needle and Black, outline the Peapod circles with a running stitch.

With tapestry needle and Black, create a French Knot (see p. 113) in the center of the Peapod circle.

Fold lion's ear at Ridge Row with WS together to create a 2-sided ear. Sew seams closed and sew ear to top of head using photograph for placement. Rep for opposite ear.

Cut 20–25 pieces of Sand and 10–15 pieces of Brown Bear each approx 8 in. to 10 in. long for lion's mane. Hold 2 strands of yarn together and fold strands in half. Using a crochet hook, insert the hook under a st near the ears, hook the 2 strands of folded yarn in the middle, and pull partway through the st. Pass the yarn ends through the loop formed, then pull to secure.

Continue around base of ears and around the entire mitten, evenly spacing the mane and alternating the 2 colors.

Prickly
PORCUPINE
MITTENS

Usually porcupines are pests, but these two have
very soft quills, are very friendly, and will happily keep
any little one's hands warm as toast!

SIZING

Measured from base of ribbing to tip of fingers:

Small (5 in.)

Large (6 in.)

Figures for larger size are given below in
parentheses. Where only one set of figures
appears, the directions apply to both sizes.

YARN

DK weight/light worsted weight yarn

The mittens shown are made with Plymouth
Yarn DK Merino Superwash: 100% fine
superwash merino wool, 1.75 oz. (50 g)/
130 yd. (119 m).

YARDAGE

50 (80) yd. DK Merino Superwash #1020
Butter

3 yd. DK Merino Superwash #1118 Dark Grey

3 yd. DK Merino Superwash #1117 Light Grey

3 yd. DK Merino Superwash #1050 Black

Small amounts of fingering or DK weight
orange scrap yarn

MATERIALS

Four U.S. size 5 double-pointed needles

Tapestry needle

Stitch markers

Stitch holder

Crochet hook

GAUGE

22 sts = 4 in.

DIRECTIONS FOR MITTENS

CUFF

With dpns and Butter, CO 30 (38) sts and
divide sts evenly onto 3 needles.

Place a st marker on right needle and, beginning
Rnd 1, join CO sts together making sure that
sts do not become twisted on needle.

P1 rnd.

Work in K2, P1 ribbing for 2 in.

K3 rnds.

GUSSET

NEXT RND (INC): (K1f&b) twice, place a second
marker, K to end of rnd.

Work 2 rnds even in St st.

NEXT RND (INC): *K1f&b, K2, K1f&b, sl marker, K
to end of rnd.

K1 rnd.*

Rep from * to *, inc 2 sts for thumb gusset
on each inc rnd, until there are 12 (14) sts
between the markers.

K first thumb st, then sl this st onto the end of
the dpn in your right hand that holds the
body sts. Sl next 10 (12) sts onto st holder.

CO 2 (3) sts. K these 2 (3) sts, K the last thumb
st, and K to end of rnd—32 (41) sts.

Work even until work measures 4 (5) in.

Divide work onto 2 dpns. The small size should
have 16 sts on each needle. The large size
should have 20 sts on one needle and 21 sts
on the second needle.

MITTEN TOP TRIANGLE

Working back and forth on 16 (20) sts:

DEC ROW: *SSK, K to last 2 sts, K2tog.

NEXT ROW: Work even in St st.

Rep these 2 rows until 4 sts remain. Place sts
on st holder.

Rep from *, working back and forth on the
16 (21) sts on second dpn to create the
opposite side of the mitten.

With WS facing, and using the Three-Needle
Bind-Off (see p. 114), BO the 5 sts at tip of
each mitten triangle.

THUMB

Transfer thumb sts from holder to 2 dpns. K
first rnd, evenly picking up 5 sts around base
of thumb for a total of 15 (17) sts for thumb.
Work even until thumb measures 1½ in. long.

THUMB RND 1 (DEC): *K2tog, K2; rep from *
around.

K1 rnd.

THUMB RND 3 (DEC): *K2tog; rep from * around. Cut yarn, leaving a 6-in. tail. Thread tail through tapestry needle and sts on needle. Pull tightly and secure on WS of work.

FINISHING

With tapestry needle and Black, create 2 French Knots (see p. 113) for 2 eyes and a nose on each mitten top.

With tapestry needle and orange scrap yarn, sew small running sts around each eye on each mitten top. Sew small running sts for smile on each mitten bottom.

Sew sides of mitten top and bottom together.

Weave in all loose ends.

Cut 20–25 pieces each of Light Grey, Dark Grey, and Black, each approx 8 in. to 10 in. long, for porcupine quills. Beginning about ½ in. from the top of the cuff ribbing, attach the quills as follows:

Hold 2 strands of yarn together and fold strands in half. Using a crochet hook, insert the hook under a st, hook the 2 strands of folded yarn in the middle and pull partway through the st. Pass the yarn ends through the loop formed, then pull to secure.

Keeping approx 2 rows between placements, work 1 row of Black, 1 row of Light Grey, and 1 row of Dark Grey. Rep until approx 20 sts from tip of mitten remain. End with 1 Black row.

OPTIONAL: Cut first Black quills a bit shorter to keep the quills from hiding ribbing. Cut remaining quills to desired lengths.

Dancing
DINOSAUR CAP

This fearsome dino just wants to dance, dance, dance!
This dino will devour the cold—and just might inspire
a dance party while she's at it.

SIZING

Small (16-in. circumference)
Large (18-in. circumference)
Figures for larger size are given below in
parentheses. Where only one set of
figures appears, the directions apply
to both sizes.

YARN

DK weight/light worsted weight yarn
The cap shown is made with Lion Brand
LB Collection Superwash Merino:
100% superwash merino wool, 3.5 oz.
(100 g)/306 yd. (280 m).

YARDAGE

40 (75) yd. Superwash Merino
#141 Wild Berry
30 yd. Superwash Merino
#174 Spring Leaf
Small amounts of fingering or DK weight
bright red, yellow, and black scrap yarn

MATERIALS

16-in. U.S. size 5 circular needle
Four U.S. size 5 double-pointed needles
One pair U.S. size 5 straight needles
Stitch marker
Tapestry needle
Small amount of polyester filling

GAUGE

24 sts = 4 in.

DIRECTIONS FOR CAP

CAP BASE

With circ needle and Wild Berry, CO 100
(120) sts. Place a st marker on right needle
and, beginning Rnd 1, join CO sts together
making sure that sts do not become
twisted on needle.
P1 rnd.
K all rnds until entire piece measures 7 (9) in.
NEXT RND: *K2tog; rep from * around.
Rep this rnd once.
BO all sts.
Cut yarn, leaving a 6-in. tail. With tapestry
needle, weave in loose end.

HEAD

With straight needles and Spring Green, CO 6 sts.

ROW 1 (RS): K1f&b into each st—12 sts.

ROW 2 (AND ALL EVEN ROWS): P.

ROW 3: (K1, K1f&b) 6 times—18 sts.

ROW 5: (K2, K1f&b) 6 times—24 sts.

ROW 7: (K3, K1f&b) 6 times—30 sts.

ROW 9: (K4, K1f&b) 6 times—36 sts.

ROW 11: (K5, K1f&b) 6 times—42 sts.

ROW 13: (K6, K1f&b) 6 times—48 sts.

Work 11 rows in St st.

SNOUT

ROW 1: (K6, K2tog) 6 times—42 sts.

ROW 2 (AND ALL EVEN ROWS): P.

ROW 3: (K5, K2tog) 6 times—36 sts.

ROW 5: (K4, K2tog) 6 times—30 sts.

ROW 7: (K3, K2tog) 6 times—24 sts.

Work 11 rows in St st.

POINTY NOSE

ROW 1: (K2, K2tog)
    6 times—18 sts.

Work 3 rows in St st.

ROW 5: (K1, K2tog)
    6 times—12 sts.

ROW 6: P.

ROW 7: (K2tog) 6 times—
    6 sts.

Cut yarn, leaving a 12-in. tail.
    Thread a tapestry needle
    and pass it through the
    remaining sts on the
    needle. Pull tightly and
    secure.

knitting tip

Any bright colors of scrap yarn will work for embroidering the face of the dinosaur. Dig through your stash and see what you can find!

ARMS

(MAKE 2)

With straight needles and Spring Green, CO 4 sts.

ROW 1: K1f&b into each st—8 sts.

ROW 2 (AND ALL EVEN ROWS): P.

ROW 3: (K1, K1f&b) 4 times—12 sts.

ROW 5: (K2, K1f&b) 4 times—16 sts.

Work 7 rows in St st.

NEXT ROW: (K2, K2tog) 4 times—12 sts.

Work 3 rows in St st.

NEXT ROW: (K1, K2tog) 4 times—8 sts.

Work 5 rows in St st.

CLAWS

*K4, turn, and work on these sts only.

NEXT ROW: P.

NEXT ROW: (K2tog) 2 times—2 sts.

NEXT ROW: P.

NEXT ROW: K2tog.

Cut yarn, leaving a 6-in. tail. Thread a tapestry needle and pass it through the remaining st on the needle. Pull tightly and secure.

With RS facing, rejoin yarn to last 4 sts and rep from * once more.

SPINE

With straight needles and Spring Green, CO 30 sts.

K1 row.

PICOT PATTERN: BO 3 sts, *CO 2 sts on left needle, BO 4 sts; rep from * to last st. Fasten off.

FINISHING

With red scrap yarn, create a smile and eyebrows by using a tapestry needle to embroider a running st across the snout and forehead.

With yellow scrap yarn, embroider a running st vertically to create teeth.

With the tapestry needle and black scrap yarn, create eyes with French Knots (see p. 113). Rep with yellow scrap yarn to create nose.

Sew up the under seam of the head, leaving a hole for stuffing. Stuff firmly with polyester filling and sew the opening closed.

Cut eight 6-in. strands of Wild Berry for hair and, using a tapestry needle, pull each strand halfway through the top of the head. Pull strands until they are even, then tie a knot. Trim hair to desired length.

Thread tapestry needle with Spring Green. Using a running stitch, attach the head securely to the top of the hat. To prevent the head from bobbing around, attach the bottom of the chin to the hat approx 2 in. from top of hat.

Attach arms to each side of the hat at desired height from the base of the hat.

Attach the spine to the back of the hat, curving and shaping as desired.

WATER

Serrated
SHARK
MITTENS AND HAT

Take a bite out of winter with these sharp-toothed shark mittens! The giant serrated mouth of the shark will keep any small fry's head warm.

Serrated Shark Mittens

SIZING

Measured from base of ribbing to tip of fingers:
Small (7 in.)
Large (8½ in.)
Figures for larger size are given below in parentheses. Where only one set of figures appears, the directions apply to both sizes.

YARN

DK weight/light worsted weight yarn
The mittens shown are made with Plymouth Yarn DK Merino Superwash: 100% fine merino superwash wool, 1.75 oz. (50 g)/130 yd. (119 m).

YARDAGE

130 (150) yd. DK Merino Superwash #1117 Light Grey
30 (40) yd. DK Merino Superwash #1126 Tangerine
3 yd. DK Merino Superwash #1000 White
3 yd. DK Merino Superwash #1050 Black

MATERIALS

One pair U.S. size 5 straight needles
Four U.S. size 5 double-pointed needles
Tapestry needle
Stitch markers
Stitch holder

GAUGE

22 sts = 4 in.

SEED STITCH

RND 1: *K1, P1; rep from * to end of rnd.
ALL OTHER RNDS: K the P sts and P the K sts.

DIRECTIONS FOR MITTENS

MOUTH AND BODY

With straight needles and Tangerine, CO 13 (20) sts.

Work St st for 4 rows.

ROW 5 (INC) (RS): *K1f&b, K to last st, K1f&b.

ROW 6: P.

Rep Rows 5 and 6 until there are 21 (26) sts on needle.*

K1 row. P1 row.

NEXT ROW (DEC): SSK, K to last 2 sts, K2tog.

NEXT ROW: P.

Rep these 2 rows until 3 (4) sts remain.

P1 row.

Cut Tangerine and attach Light Grey.

K1 row. P1 row.

Rep from * to *.

P1 row.

NEXT ROW (DEC): SSK, K to last 2 sts, K2tog.

NEXT ROW: P.

Rep these 2 rows until there are 17 (22) sts.

Work 3 rows in St st.

Transfer sts onto st holder.

Rep these instructions to make another identical piece, but when completed, leave sts on needle.

With Light Grey, work St st across 17 (22) sts on needle. Place sts from st holder onto needle and work across 17 (22) sts of first piece— 34 (44) sts.

Divide sts evenly onto 3 dpns and place marker to mark the beginning of the rnd.

RND 1: K17 (22), place marker, K to end of rnd.

Work 3 rnds in St st.

RND 5 (INC): K1f&b, K to second marker, sl marker, K1f&b, K to end of rnd.

RND 6: K.

Rep these 2 rows until there are 50 (60) sts.

Cont working in the rnd until piece measures 6 (8) in. from point of Light Grey nose.

Work K1, P1 ribbing for 1½ in. BO all sts.

FIN

(MAKE 2)

With straight needles and Light Grey, CO 20 (30) sts.

Work in Seed st for 2 rows.

ROW 3 (DEC): SSK, K to last 2 sts, K2tog.

ROW 4: Work in Seed st.

Rep Rows 3 and 4 until 4 sts remain.

NEXT ROW: SSK, K2tog.

BO all sts.

FINISHING

With tapestry needle and Light Grey, fold Tangerine linings to inside of shark's mouth and sew with small running stitches.

With tapestry needle and Tangerine, sew cast-on edges of mouth lining to close opening at back of shark's mouth.

With tapestry needle and White, create French Knots (see p. 113) for small teeth on top and bottom of mouth.

With tapestry needle and Black, create French Knots for shark eyes.

With tapestry needle and Light Grey, sew 2 fins together and then sew completed fin to back center of mitten.

Weave in all loose ends.

knitting tip

How many times have you created one mitten from a set, only to lose inspiration and never make the second? Work both at the same time to stay motivated.

Serrated Shark Hat

SIZING
One size (16-in. circumference)

YARN
DK weight/light worsted weight yarn
The hat shown is made with Plymouth Yarn
    DK Merino Superwash: 100% fine merino
    superwash wool, 1.75 oz. (50 g)/130 yd.
    (119 m).

YARDAGE
130 yd. DK Merino Superwash #1117 Light Grey
40 yd. DK Merino Superwash #1104 Firecracker
20 yd. DK Merino Superwash #1000 White
5 yd. DK Merino Superwash #1050 Black

MATERIALS
16-in. U.S. size 5 circular needle
Four U.S. size 5 double-pointed needles
One pair U.S. size 5 straight needles
Stitch marker
Tapestry needle
Stitch holders

GAUGE
22 sts = 4 in.

SEED STITCH
RND 1: *K1, P1; rep from * to end of rnd.
ALL OTHER RNDS: K the P sts and P the K sts.

DIRECTIONS FOR HAT

MOUTH
(MAKE 2)
With straight needles and Light Grey, CO 6 sts.
ROW 1 (INC): K1f&b, work even in Seed st to last
    st, K1f&b.
ROW 2: Work even in Seed st.
Rep these 2 rows until you have 40 sts on
    needle. Place all sts on holder and rep for
    second flap.

MOUTH LINING
(MAKE 2)
With straight needles and Firecracker, rep
    instructions for mouth, creating 2 more
    flaps for lining.

HAT BODY

Transfer the 2 Light Grey sets of sts from holder onto circ needle. You should have 80 sts on needle.

Placing a st marker at beginning of rnd, work in St st until piece measures 3 in. from beginning of St st.

NEXT RND (DEC): *K8, K2tog; rep from * to end of rnd.

K5 rnds.

NEXT RND (DEC): *K7, K2tog; rep from * to end of rnd.

K4 rnds.

NEXT RND (DEC): *K6, K2tog; rep from * to end of rnd.

K4 rnds.

NEXT RND (DEC): *K5, K2tog; rep from * to end of rnd.

K3 rnds.

NEXT RND (DEC): *K4, K2tog; rep from * to end of rnd.

K3 rnds.

NEXT RND (DEC): *K3, K2tog; rep from * to end of rnd.

TAIL FINS

Divide remaining sts onto 2 dpns, placing 14 sts on one needle and 18 sts on the second needle.

Working 1 set of sts at a time and working back and forth in St st, work 2 rnds.

NEXT RND (DEC): SSK, work St st to last 2 sts, K2tog.

NEXT RND: Work even in St st.

Rep these 2 rows until 2 sts remain. BO all sts.

Cut yarn, leaving an 8-in. tail. Rep with second set of sts, creating 1 small fin and 1 large fin.

TAIL FIN LINING

(MAKE 1 SMALL AND 1 LARGE)

SMALL

With straight needles and Light Grey, CO 14 sts. Work 2 rows in St st.

NEXT ROW: SSK, work St st to last 2 sts, K2tog.

Rep these 2 rows until 2 sts remain. BO all sts. Cut yarn, leaving an 8-in. tail.

LARGE

With straight needles and Light Grey, CO 18 sts. Work same as Small.

FIN

NOTE: Entire fin is worked in Seed st.

With straight needles and Light Grey, CO 3 sts.

ROW 1: K1f&b, work in Seed st to last st, K1f&b.

ROW 2: Work even in Seed st.

Rep these 2 rows until there are 15 sts.

NEXT ROW (INC): K1f&b, work in Seed st to end of row.

NEXT ROW: Work even in Seed st.

Rep these 2 rows until there are 20 sts, ending after the inc row.

RIDGE ROW: K.

NEXT ROW (DEC): SSK, work in Seed st to end of row.

NEXT ROW: Work even in Seed st.

Rep these 2 rows until there are 15 sts. Cut yarn, leaving a 12-in. tail.

TEETH

(MAKE 12)

With White and straight needles, CO 9 sts. Work 1 row in Garter st. Dec 1 st each end every other rnd until 2 sts remain. BO all sts.

FINISHING

Place small tail fin and small tail fin lining WS together. Use yarn tail to sew lining to fin using a small running stitch. Rep for large tail fin and large tail fin lining.

With tapestry needle and Light Grey, sew top of hat closed using a small running st, letting both fins fall to each side of hat.

With tapestry needle and Firecracker, sew shark's mouth lining onto inside of shark's mouth.

Fold fin in half at Ridge Row and thread a tapestry needle with the yarn tail. Using a running st, sew fin closed. Using the same yarn tail and photo for placement, attach fin in the middle of one side of hat with elongated end toward top.

With tapestry needle and White, sew teeth onto inside of each side of earflaps.

With tapestry needle and Black, use Duplicate Stitch (see p. 113) to create 2 large circles for shark's eyes above mouth right under the shark's fin.

Weave in all loose ends.

knitting tip

When your little one wants to play outside, just rotate this hat so that the two halves of the shark's mouth become earflaps for an even toastier accessory!

Jumbo CRAB CAP

With two enormous claws and googly eyes, this crab cap is almost good enough to eat, but please leave it on top of your little one's head!

SIZING

Small (16-in. circumference)

Large (19-in. circumference)

Figures for larger size are given below in parentheses. Where only one set of figures appears, the directions apply to both sizes.

YARN

Worsted weight, single-ply yarn

The cap shown is made with Classic Elite MinnowMerino: 100% extra-fine superwash merino, 1.75 oz. (50 g)/77 yd. (70 m).

YARDAGE

70 (90) yd. MinnowMerino #4758 Rogue

25 yd. MinnowMerino #4701 Snow White

Small amount of fingering or DK weight black scrap yarn

MATERIALS

16-in. U.S. size 8 circular needle

One pair U.S. size 8 straight needles

Four U.S. size 8 double-pointed needles

Tapestry needle

Stitch marker

One 12-in. pipe cleaner (optional)

GAUGE

18 sts = 4 in.

DIRECTIONS FOR HAT

HAT BASE

With Rogue and circ needle, CO 70 (80) sts. Place a st marker on right needle and, beginning Rnd 1, join CO sts together making sure that sts do not become twisted on needle.

P1 rnd.

K all rnds until entire piece measures 4 (5) in.

RIDGE RND: P.

*knitting tip

It's easy to add support to the claw arms. Just work your I-cord around a pipe cleaner for added stability. This will also allow you to shape the arms as you see fit.

HAT CROWN

K5 rnds.

NEXT RND (DEC): *K8, K2tog; rep from * for entire rnd.

NEXT RND (DEC): *K7, K2tog; rep from * for entire rnd.

Continue in established pattern, knitting 1 less st between decs and switching to dpns when necessary, until you have approx 4 sts on needle.

Cut yarn, leaving a 6-in. tail. With tapestry needle, thread the tail through the remaining sts on the needle. Secure the tail on the WS of the work.

JUMBO CLAWS

(MAKE 4)

With Rogue and straight needles, CO 14 sts.

ROW 1: P.

ROW 2: K.

ROW 3: K.

ROW 4: P.

ROW 5: SSK, K to last 2 sts on needle, K2tog.

ROW 6: P.

Divide work.

*ROW 7: SSK, K5, turn work.

ROW 8: Working on these 6 sts only, P.

ROW 9: P.

ROW 10: SSK, K4.

ROW 11: P.

ROW 12: SSK, K3.

ROW 13: P.

ROW 14: SSK, K1.*

BO.

For opposite side of claw, attach yarn to the RS on remaining sts and rep from * to *.

NOTE: Using pipe cleaners inside the I-Cord will make the claw arm squiggle even more!

OPTIONAL: Cut a 12-in. pipe cleaner in half. With one 6-in. piece, and holding it perpendicular to dpn, simply work the I-Cord around the pipe cleaner to easily enclose the pipe cleaner inside.

FINISHING

With tapestry needle and Rogue, sew each claw together with WS facing, using a running stitch. Attach I-Cords to center bottom of each claw. Attach I-Cord securely to WS of cap Ridge Row using I-Cord tails. With tapestry needle, attach one side of bottom of claw to cap to help keep the claw sticking out.

With tapestry needle and Rogue, sew small running stitches around the circumference of each eye. With black scrap yarn, create a large French Knot (see p. 113) in the center of each eye.

Sew googly eyes to crown of cap.

Weave in all loose ends.

GOOGLY EYES

(MAKE 4)

Using Snow White and straight needles, CO 5 sts.

ROW 1: P.

ROW 2 (INC): K to last st, K1f&b.

Rep these 2 rows until 11 sts remain.

Work 2 rows even in St st.

Dec 1 st each end of every other row until 5 sts remain.

BO all sts.

CLAW ARMS

Using Rogue, create an I-Cord (see p. 114) approx 7 in. long. Cut yarn, leaving a 3-in. tail. Thread tapestry needle and pass through sts on needle. Work tapestry needle through the entire cord until you have both the CO tail and the working tail on the same end of cord.

knitting tip

* Join the group! Always try to join new yarn at the beginning of a row. A simple slip knot around the existing yarn will let you untie later to weave in those loose ends.

JUMBO CRAB CAP **55**

Enormous
ANEMONE HAT

This sea urchin has many terrestrial flowers decorating the tip of the crown, creating a wild and wonderful hat. Gentle ocean waves decorate the brim.

SIZING

Small (16-in. circumference)

Large (20-in. circumference)

Figures for larger size are given below in parentheses. Where only one set of figures appears, the directions apply to both sizes.

YARN

DK weight smooth yarn

The hat shown is made with Westminster Fibers S.R. Kertzer Super 10 Cotton: 100% mercerized cotton, 4.4 oz. (125 g)/250 yd. (229 m).

YARDAGE

60 (80) yd. Super 10 Cotton #3532 Soft Yellow

20 yd. Super 10 Cotton #3446 Cotton Candy

10 yd. Super 10 Cotton #3841 Caribbean

MATERIALS

16-in. U.S. size 4 circular needle

Five U.S. size 4 double-pointed needles

Stitch marker

Tapestry needle

GAUGE

22 sts = 4 in.

DIRECTIONS FOR HAT

HAT BASE

With circ needles and Soft Yellow, CO 80 (100) sts. Place a st marker on right needle and, beginning Rnd 1, join CO sts together making sure that sts do not become twisted on needle.

P1 rnd.

K each rnd until entire piece measures 3½ in.

P1 rnd.

K5 rnds.

NEXT RND (DEC): *K8, K2tog; rep from * to end of rnd.

NEXT RND (DEC): *K7, K2tog; rep from * to end of rnd.

Continue in established pattern, knitting 1 less st between decs and switching to dpns when necessary, until you have approx 5 sts.

Cut yarn, leaving a 6-in. tail. Thread a tapestry needle and pass through remaining sts on needle. Bring yarn to WS of work and secure.

TERRESTRIAL FLOWERS
(MAKE 15)

Using dpns and Soft Yellow, CO 6 sts.

Work I-Cord (see p. 114) for 4 rows.

K2tog at beg and end of next row—4 sts.

Cut Soft Yellow and attach Cotton Candy.

Work I-Cord for 4 rows.

K2tog at beg and end of next row—2 sts.

Continue in I-Cord for another 4 rows.

Cut yarn, leaving a 6-in. tail. Thread a tapestry needle and pass through remaining 2 sts. Carefully work yarn tail down center of entire piece. Sew side seams at beginning of flower. Use all yarn tails at the base of the flower to attach flower to hat.

FINISHING

Using photograph for placement, attach Terrestrial Flowers around crown of hat, letting them fall at different angles.

With tapestry needle and Caribbean, use Duplicate Stitch (see p. 113) to create waves of the ocean all along the base of the hat.

knitting tip

Love the flowers that sit atop this hat? Don't stop at just 15! Make as many flowers as you'd like to make the hat even wilder.

Puckering
CLOWN FISH CAP

This clown fish likes to flutter all around,
keeping any baby's head as warm as the
Indian Ocean it likes to swim in!

SIZING

One size (19-in. circumference)

YARN

Worsted weight, single-ply yarn
The hat shown is made with Classic Elite
    MinnowMerino: 100% extra-fine superwash
    merino, 1.75 oz. (50 g)/77 yd. (70 m).

YARDAGE

70 yd. MinnowMerino #4785 Orangini
30 yd. MinnowMerino #4701 Snow White
20 yd. DK weight black scrap yarn

MATERIALS

16-in. U.S. size 8 circular needle
One pair U.S. size 8 straight needles
Four U.S. size 8 double-pointed needles
Tapestry needle
Stitch markers

GAUGE

18 sts = 4 in. with MinnowMerino

SEED STITCH

RND 1: *K1, P1: rep from * to end of rnd.
ALL OTHER RNDS: K the P sts and P the K sts.

DIRECTIONS FOR CAP

CAP BASE

With Orangini and circ needle, CO 80 sts. Place
    a st marker on right needle and, beginning
    Rnd 1, join CO sts together making sure that
    sts do not become twisted on needle.
RIDGE RND: *P1 rnd.
K5 rnds.*
Rep from * to * once, then rep Ridge Rnd once
    more.
NEXT RND: K40, place marker, K40.
NEXT RND (DEC): Work to 2 sts before marker
    at halfway point, SSK, sl marker, K1, K2tog,
    work to 2 sts before second marker at
    beginning of rnd, SSK, sl marker, K1, K2tog,
    and continue the second rnd with no decs.
    You will dec at each marker every other time
    you reach the markers. Rep these decs until
    74 sts remain.
K2 rnds.

STRIPE ROUNDS

NOTE: Cont to slip markers as you work these rnds.

Drop Orangini and attach black scrap yarn. K1 rnd.

Drop black and attach Snow White. K2 rnds.

Cut Snow White and pick up black. K1 rnd.

Cut black and pick up Orangini. Work 12 rnds.

Drop Orangini and attach black. K1 rnd.

Drop black and attach Snow White. K8 rnds.

Cut Snow White.

With Orangini, work dec rnd every rnd at each marker, placing sts on dpns when necessary, until 24 sts remain. Remove markers.

Drop Orangini and attach black. K1 rnd.

Drop black and attach Snow White. K2 rnds.

Cut Snow White and pick up black. K1 rnd.

Cut black and pick up Orangini. K3 rnds. BO all sts.

FIN

(MAKE 2 SMALL AND 2 LARGE)

NOTE: Directions for large fin are in parentheses.

*knitting tip

Clown fish can be found in all sorts of colors. Be creative with your choice of yarns!

With Orangini and straight needles, CO
15 (20) sts. Work in Seed st for 2 rows.

DEC ROW: SSK, work Seed st to last 2 sts,
K2tog.

Continue Dec Row every other row until
9 (8) sts remain. BO all sts.

FINISHING

With tapestry needle and black scrap
yarn, outline the end of each fin
using the Blanket Stitch (see p. 112).

Attach large fins to each side of clown
fish, then attach second smaller fin on
top of large fins.

With tapestry needle and Snow White,
create eyes on each side of hat top using
Duplicate Stitch (see p. 113) and referring to
the photograph for placement. With black,
outline each eye and place a French Knot
(see p. 113) in the center.

Fold bottom of hat under toward WS at Ridge
Rnd and sew neatly in place with tapestry
needle.

Weave in all loose ends.

Barnacle
STARFISH BERET

A sweet and sassy sea star for your little star—
complete with barnacles! This winter hat will remind you
of summer trips to the beach.

SIZING

Small (16-in. circumference)
Large (19-in. circumference)
Figures for larger size are given below in
parentheses. Where only one set of figures
appears, the directions apply to both sizes.

YARN

Worsted weight, single-ply yarn
The beret shown is made with Classic Elite
MinnowMerino: 100% extra-fine superwash
merino, 1.75 oz. (50 g)/77 yd. (70 m).

YARDAGE

40 (50) yd. MinnowMerino #4757 Bluette
40 (50) yd. MinnowMerino #4735 Chartreuse
30 (40) yd. MinnowMerino #4704 Icy Blue
20 yd. MinnowMerino #4750 Goldie

MATERIALS

16-in. U.S. size 8 circular needle
One pair U.S. size 8 straight needles
Four U.S. size 8 double-pointed needles
Stitch marker
Tapestry needle

GAUGE

18 sts = 4 in.

DIRECTIONS FOR BERET

BERET BASE

With Bluette and circ needles, CO 72 (80)
sts. Place a st marker on right needle and,
beginning Rnd 1, join CO sts together making
sure that sts do not become twisted on
needle.
P1 rnd.
Work K2, P1 ribbing for 1½ in.
RIDGE RNDS: K1 rnd. P1 rnd.

knitting tip

French knots (p. 113) are easy to make and are my all-time favorite way to add color, texture, and fun to any project.

STARFISH POINTS

Cut Bluette and attach Icy Blue.

RND 1: K, using st markers to divide work into 4 equal parts, every 18 (20) sts.

RND 2 (INC): *K to 1 st before first marker, K1f&b, sl marker, K to 1 st before next marker, K1f&b; rep from * to end of rnd.

Work 10 more inc rnds.

RIDGE RND: Cut Icy Blue and attach Chartreuse.

K1 rnd. P1 rnd.

DECREASE ROUNDS

At each marker, make the following dec on each rnd, placing sts on dpns when necessary:

Work to 2 sts before marker, SSK, sl marker, K1, K2tog.

Cont working dec rnd until you have 4–6 sts on needle. Cut yarn, leaving a 6-in. tail. Thread a tapestry needle with tail and pass through remaining sts on needle. Pass needle to WS of work and fasten off.

FINISHING

With tapestry needle and Goldie, create French
    Knot (see p. 113) barnacles around each Icy
    Blue side.
With tapestry needle and Bluette, make
    diagonal decorative threads on each
    starfish point.

cantankerous
CROCODILE
HAT AND SCARF

This big-eyed crocodile will wrap itself around any little one's head for an easy topper. Crocodiles are very sensitive to cold, so create the comfy matching scarf to keep your little one warm.

Cantankerous Crocodile Hat

SIZING

One size (17-in. circumference)

YARN

Worsted weight, single-ply yarn
The cap shown is made with Classic Elite MinnowMerino: 100% extra-fine superwash merino, 1.75 oz. (50 g)/77 yd. (70 m).

YARDAGE

100 yd. MinnowMerino #4735 Chartreuse
10 yd. MinnowMerino #4750 Goldie
Small amount of fingering or DK weight black scrap yarn

MATERIALS

One pair U.S. size 8 straight needles
Tapestry needle
Two U.S. size 8 double-pointed needles
Crochet hook

GAUGE

18 sts = 4 in.

SEED STITCH

ROW 1: *K1, P1; rep from * to end of row.
ALL OTHER ROWS: K the P sts and P the K sts.

DIRECTIONS FOR HAT

BUMPY CROCODILE PATTERN

With Chartreuse and straight needles, CO 24 sts.

ROW 1 (RS): K.

ROW 2: K1, P22, K1.

ROW 3: K1, P1, *(K5, turn, P5, turn) 3 times, K5*, P10, rep from * to * to last 2 sts, P1, K1.

ROW 4: K2, P5, K10, P5, K2.

ROW 5: K.

ROW 6: K1, P22, K1.

ROW 7: K1, P5, *(K5, turn, P5, turn) 3 times, K5*, P2, rep from * to *, P5, K1.

ROW 8: K6, P5, K2, P5, K6.

Rep these 8 rows until entire piece measures 8 in.

FRONT BRIM

Work Seed st for 3 in.

Continuing to work in Seed st, K2tog at beg and end of every other row until 10–15 sts remain. BO all sts.

Fold Seed st brim at first dec toward RS of work and carefully sew in place.

CAP SIDES

With straight needles and RS facing, pick up 30 sts along one side of Bumpy Crocodile Pattern. Work Seed st for 3½ in. BO all sts.

Rep for opposite side of cap.

FINISHING

With Chartreuse and dpns, CO 3 sts for chin tie. Create two I-Cords (see p. 114) approx 12 in. long. With crochet hook, carefully weave in I-Cord at the base of each side piece to create a cinch so that the cap can curve easily around your little one's head. Make a medium-size knot in the I-Cord at the back of the hat to secure it. Leave enough of the I-Cord tails to easily create a large bow at the front of the cap to tie under the chin.

With Goldie and straight needles, CO 8 sts for eyes. Working in Seed st, work approx 8 rows or until you have created a square. Cut yarn, leaving a 6-in. tail. Thread a tapestry needle and pass it through the sts on the needle, then sew a running st along the other 3 sides of the square. Pull tightly until you have created a ball. Secure all loose ends. Thread a tapestry needle with black scrap yarn and create a French Knot (see p. 113) in the middle of the eye.

Rep to create a second eye.

* knitting tip

Fix it when you find it! If you find an error a few rows back, stop and fix it right away. Otherwise, later, you'll wish you did.

Cantankerous Crocodile Scarf

SIZING
One size (36 in. long)

YARN
Worsted weight, single-ply yarn
The scarf shown is made with Classic Elite MinnowMerino: 100% extra-fine superwash merino, 1.75 oz. (50 g)/77 yd. (70 m).

YARDAGE
230 yd. MinnowMerino #4735 Chartreuse

MATERIALS
One pair U.S. size 8 needles
Tapestry needle

GAUGE
18 sts = 4 in.

SEED STITCH
ROW 1: *K1, P1: rep from * to end of row.
ALL OTHER ROWS: K the P sts and P the K sts.

MAKE BOBBLE (MB)
Knit into the front and back of the stitch twice, then once more into the front. Drop the st from your left needle. Turn work and P across the 5 sts. Turn work and BO kwise until 1 st remains.

DIRECTIONS FOR SCARF

BUMPY CROCODILE PATTERN

With Chartreuse and straight needles,
CO 24 sts.

ROW 1 (RS): K.

ROW 2: K1, P22, K1.

ROW 3: K1, P1, *(K5, turn, P5, turn) 3 times, K5*,
P10, rep from * to * to last 2 sts, P1, K1.

ROW 4: K2, P5, K10, P5, K2.

ROW 5: K.

ROW 6: K1, P22, K1.

ROW 7: K1, P5, *(K5, turn, P5, turn) 3 times, K5*,
P2, rep from * to *, P5, K1.

ROW 8: K6, P5, K2, P5, K6.

Rep these 8 rows until entire piece measures
8 in.

HEAD

Work Seed st for 4 rows.

DEC ROW: SSK, work in Seed st to last 2 sts,
K2tog.

Work 4 rows in Seed st.

Rep Dec Row.

Work 1 row in Seed st.

EYES

Working in Seed st, work 5 sts, MB, work 8 sts,
MB, work 5 sts.

Work 2 rows in Seed st.

Work Dec Row as for head.

Work 4 rows in Seed st.

BO all sts.

TAIL

CO 16 sts and work Seed st for 10 rows.

*Work Dec Row as for head.

Work in Seed st for 4 rows.*

Rep from * to * until 8 sts remain.

Work in Seed st for 4 rows.

BO all sts.

FINISHING

Using a tapestry needle and placing RS
together, sew tail to end of scarf using a
small running stitch.

Weave in all loose ends.

Prideful
POLAR BEAR
SNOW CAP

A symbol of the Arctic, this polar bear has a huge nose—and a huge smile. Poking his head up from his blue iceberg, he'll keep any head warm and cozy.

SIZING

Small (16-in. circumference)

Large (19-in. circumference)

Figures for larger size are given below in parentheses. Where only one set of figures appears, the directions apply to both sizes.

YARN

Worsted weight, single-ply yarn

The hat shown is made with Classic Elite MinnowMerino: 100% extra-fine superwash merino, 1.75 oz. (50 g)/77 yd. (70 m).

YARDAGE

60 (75) yd. MinnowMerino #4701 Snow White

50 (60) yd. MinnowMerino #4704 Icy Blue

10 yd. MinnowMerino #4713 Jet Black

MATERIALS

16-in. U.S. size 8 circular needle

One pair U.S. size 8 straight needles

Four U.S. size 8 double-pointed needles

Tapestry needle

Stitch marker

Small amount of polyester filling

GAUGE

18 sts = 4 in.

DIRECTIONS FOR CAP

CAP BASE

With Icy Blue and circ needle, CO 70 (80) sts. Place a st marker on right needle and, beginning Rnd 1, join CO sts together making sure that sts do not become twisted on needle.

P1 rnd.

Work K2, P1 ribbing for 2 in.

Cut Icy Blue and attach Snow White.

K all rnds until piece measures 2 in. from top of ribbing.

NOSE

RND 1 (INC): K35 (40), place marker, K1f&b, K1, K1f&b, place second marker, K to end of rnd.

RND 2 (INC): K to marker, sl marker, K1f&b, K to st before second marker, K1f&b, sl marker, K to end of rnd.

Continue in St st, working the inc rnd until you have 19 sts between nose markers.

Work 4 rows even in St st.

NEXT RND (DEC): K to first marker, sl marker, SSK, K to 2 sts before second marker, K2tog, sl marker, K to end of rnd.

Rep dec rnd one time, removing markers.

HAT DECREASES

NEXT ROW (DEC): *K8, K2tog; rep from * to last 5 sts, K5.

NEXT ROW (DEC): *K7, K2tog; rep from * to last 5 sts, K5.

NEXT ROW (DEC): *K6, K2tog; rep from * to last 5 sts, K5.

NEXT ROW (DEC): *K5, K2tog; rep from * to last 5 sts, K5.

NEXT ROW (DEC): *K4, K2tog; rep from * to last 5 sts, K5.

NEXT ROW (DEC): *K3, K2tog; rep from * to end of rnd.

NEXT ROW (DEC): *K2, K2tog; rep from * to end of rnd.

NEXT ROW (DEC): *K1, K2tog; rep from * to end of rnd.

K2tog entire rnd until approx 5 sts remain. Cut yarn, leaving a 6-in. tail. Thread tapestry needle and pass through sts on needle. Bring yarn to WS and secure.

EARS

(MAKE 2)

With Snow White and straight needles, CO 10 sts.

Work St st for 8 rows.

DEC ROW: SSK, work to last 2 sts, K2tog.

NEXT ROW: P.

Rep these 2 rows until 4 sts remain, ending after working a RS row.

RIDGE ROW (WS): K.

K1 row.

NEXT ROW (INC): K1f&b, K to last st, K1f&b.

NEXT ROW: P.

Rep these 2 rows until 10 sts remain on needle.

Work even in St st for 7 rows. BO all sts.

NOSE LINING

With Snow White and straight needles, CO 3 sts.

ROW 1 (INC): K1f&b, K to last st, K1f&b.
ROW 2: P.
Rep these 2 rows until there are 19 sts on
   needle.
K1 row.
P1 row.
BO all sts.

FINISHING

With Snow White and tapestry needle,
   and with the point of the nose lining
   meeting the point where the nose
   begins to inc, sew lining carefully
   into place on the WS of hat.
   Leave the top of the nose
   open for easy removal of
   stuffing. Using a small amount
   of polyester filling, stuff the
   bear's nose in the pocket
   created.

With tapestry needle
   and Jet Black, and
   using the photograph
   for placement, use
   Duplicate Stitch (see
   p. 113) to create the
   bear's smile and nose.

Fold ear together at Ridge
   Row with WS facing. With
   Snow White and tapestry
   needle, sew the 2 sides of
   each ear together. With Jet Black
   and tapestry needle, create a small
   French Knot (see p. 113) in the center of
   each ear.

With Snow White and tapestry needle, and
   using the photograph for placement, sew
   each ear carefully to the face of the bear.

coiling
SERPENT HAT

These flexible reptiles wrap themselves
nicely around to help keep this hat
on top of your little one's head.

SIZING

SMALL: 16-in. to 18-in. circumference
LARGE: 20-in. circumference
Figures for larger size are given in parentheses.
  Where only one set of figures appears, the
  directions apply to both sizes.

YARN

DK weight/light worsted weight yarn
The cap shown is made with Plymouth Yarn
  DK Merino Superwash: 100% fine superwash
  merino wool, 1.75 oz. (50 g)/130 yd. (119 m).

YARDAGE

80 (90) yd. DK Merino Superwash #1118 Dark
  Grey
40 yd. DK Merino Superwash #1123 Peapod
1 yd. DK Merino Superwash #1126 Tangerine

MATERIALS

16-in. U.S. size 5 circular needle
Two U.S. size 5 double-pointed needles
Stitch marker
Tapestry needle

GAUGE

5½ sts = 1 in

DIRECTIONS FOR CAP

HAT BASE

With circ needle and Dark Grey, CO 80 (100)
  sts. Place a st marker on right needle and,
  beginning Rnd 1, join CO sts together making
  sure that sts do not become twisted on
  needle.
P1 rnd.
K all rnds until entire piece measures 2½ in.

DECREASE ROUNDS

RND 1 (DEC): *K8, K2tog; rep from * to end of rnd.
K9 rnds.
RND 2 (DEC): *K7, K2tog; rep from * to end of rnd.
K5 rnds.
RND 3 (DEC): *K6, K2tog; rep from * to end
  of rnd.
K5 rnds.

RND 4 (DEC): *K5, K2tog; rep from * to end of rnd. K5 rnds.

RND 5 (DEC): *K4, K2tog; rep from * to end of rnd. K4 rnds.

RND 6 (DEC): *K3, K2tog; rep from * to end of rnd. K4 rnds.

RND 7 (DEC): *K2, K2tog; rep from * to end of rnd. K2 rnds.

RND 8 (DEC): *K1, K2tog; rep from * to end of rnd. K1 rnd.

K2tog entire rnd.

FINISHING THE HAT BASE

Cut yarn, leaving a 6-in. tail. Thread a tapestry needle and pass needle through remaining sts on needle. Fasten off and secure tail to WS of work.

SNAKES

Make as many as desired.

With dpns and Peapod, CO 4 sts, leaving a 10-in. tail for seaming, and work I-Cord (see p. 114) for 10 in.

NEXT ROW: K1f&b into first and last st (6 sts total). Knitting back and forth, K6 rows. K2tog, K to last 2 sts, K2tog. Return to I-Cord knitting on 4 sts. Work 4 rows. Cut yarn, leaving a 10-in. tail. Thread through last sts on needle. Fasten off.

SNAKE TONGUE

Cut a 1-in. piece of Tangerine. Thread a tapestry needle with Tangerine and pass through tip of snake. Tie a secure knot and cut the strand of yarn to desired length. Make the hat more dynamic by making each tongue a different length—some short and some long—to allude to hissing, or keep the tongues consistent if you want a more structured look.

FINISHING

Using the CO and BO tails of snakes, sew snakes to the top of the hat. This is where things get fun, because you can curl the snakes however you wish when placing them on the hat. Curl them into themselves and around each other in interesting ways to keep your little one intrigued.

knitting tip

You can knit as many snakes as you want for this hat. Fewer snakes will pop against the darker yarn of the hat base, while adding more will bring more color and motion into the mix. I knitted seven for my hat; knit as many or as few as you like.

AIR

Fabulously Fat
FLYING PIG CAP

Flying pigs are possible when your little one wears this cute fat pig cap. Onlookers will be happy to claim to have finally seen pigs flying!

SIZING

Small (16-in. circumference)

Large (19-in. circumference)

Figures for larger size are given below in parentheses. Where only one set of figures appears, the directions apply to both sizes.

YARN

Worsted weight, single-ply yarn

The cap shown is made with Classic Elite MinnowMerino: 100% extra-fine superwash merino, 1.75 oz. (50 g)/77 yd. (70 m).

YARDAGE

70 (80) yd. MinnowMerino #4719 Icy Pinque

40 yd. MinnowMerino #4701 Snow White

5 yd. MinnowMerino #4713 Jet Black

1 yd. MinnowMerino #4755 Cerise

MATERIALS

16-in. U.S. size 8 circular needle

One pair U.S. size 8 straight needles

Four U.S. size 8 double-pointed needles

Tapestry needle

Stitch markers

Small amount of polyester filling

GAUGE

18 sts = 4 in.

SEED STITCH

RND 1: *K1, P1; rep from * to end of rnd.

ALL OTHER RNDS: K the P sts and P the K sts.

DIRECTIONS FOR CAP

CAP BASE

With Icy Pinque and circ needle, CO 80 (90) sts. Place a st marker on right needle and, beginning Rnd 1, join CO sts together making sure that sts do not become twisted on needle.

P1 rnd.

Work K1, P1 ribbing for 3 rnds.

NOSE

RND 1 (INC): K40 (45), place marker, K1f&b, K1, K1f&b, place second marker, K to end of rnd.

RND 2 (INC): K to marker, sl marker, K1f&b, K to st before second marker, K1f&b, sl marker, K to end of rnd.

Continue in St st, working inc rnd until you have 19 sts between markers.

Work 4 rows even in St st.

NEXT RND (DEC): K to first marker, sl marker, SSK, K to 2 sts before second nose marker, K2tog, K to end of rnd.

Rep dec rnd one time, removing markers.

HAT DECREASES

NEXT RND: *K8, K2tog; rep from * to end of rnd.
NEXT RND: *K7, K2tog; rep from * to end of rnd.
NEXT RND: *K6, K2tog; rep from * to end of rnd.
NEXT RND: *K3, K2tog; rep from * to end of rnd.
NEXT RND: *K2, K2tog; rep from * to end of rnd.
NEXT RND: *K1, K2tog; rep from * to end of rnd.

K2tog entire rnd until approx 5 sts remain. Cut yarn, leaving a 6-in. tail. Thread tapestry needle and pass through sts on needle. Bring yarn to WS and secure.

EARS

(MAKE 2)

With Icy Pinque and straight needles, CO 10 sts.

ROW 1: P.
ROW 2 (DEC): SSK, K to end of row.
ROW 3: P.

Rep Rows 2 and 3 until 6 sts remain. BO all sts.

knitting tip

Omit the wings from this flying pig if you want the fun to stay grounded!

NOSE LINING

With Icy Pinque and straight needles, CO 3 sts.

INC ROW: K1f&b, K to last st, K1f&b.

NEXT ROW: P.

Rep these 2 rows until 27 sts remain.

K1 row.

P1 row.

BO all sts.

WINGS

(MAKE 4)

Using straight needles and Snow White, CO 20 sts.

ROW 1: Work in Seed st.

ROW 2: Work Seed st to last 2 sts, K2tog.

Rep Rows 1 and 2 until 10 sts remain.

BO all sts.

SQUIGGLE TAIL

With Icy Pinque and straight needles, CO 15 sts.

Kf&b&f into each st, creating 3 sts from 1 st.

BO all sts pwise.

FINISHING

With Icy Pinque and tapestry needle, and with the point of the nose lining meeting the point where the nose begins to inc, sew lining carefully into place on the WS of hat. Leave the top of the nose open for easy stuffing. Using a small amount of polyester filling, stuff pig's nose in the pocket created so it stands out big and proud.

With Jet Black and tapestry needle, and using the photograph for placement, create a Duplicate Stitch (see p. 113) pattern for the pig's nose and outline of smile and nose. With Cerise and tapestry needle, and using a small running stitch, make a large smile for the friendly pig.

With Icy Pinque and tapestry needle, and using the photograph for placement, sew each ear to the face of the pig.

Sew 2 wings together, placing a small amount of polyester filling in each wing to help the pig fly! Rep for second set of wings. With Snow White and tapestry needle, attach center of each wing to top center of pig.

Curl squiggle tail into a curlicue and attach to the back of the pig. Now let this fabulously fat pig take off and fly!

Beastly
BLACKBIRD HAT

Don't bake this bird in a pie! This hat will
keep your wild bird warm no matter
what weather blows your way.

SIZING

Small (16-in. circumference)

Large (18-in. circumference)

Figures for larger size are given below in
parentheses. Where only one set of figures
appears, the directions apply to both sizes.

YARN

DK weight yarn

The hat shown is made with Plymouth Yarn
DK Merino Superwash: 100% fine superwash
merino wool, 1.75 oz. (50 g)/130 yd. (119 m).

YARDAGE

100 (130) yd. DK Merino Superwash #1050
Black

5 yd. DK Merino Superwash #1108 Sunshine

1 yd. DK Merino Superwash #1104 Firecracker

MATERIALS

16-in. U.S. size 5 circular needle

One pair U.S. size 5 straight needles

Two U.S. size 5 double-pointed needles

Stitch marker

Tapestry needle

Small amount of polyester filling

GAUGE

22 sts = 4 in.

DIRECTIONS FOR HAT

HAT BASE

With circ needle and Black, CO 90 (110) sts.
Place a st marker on right needle and,
beginning Rnd 1, join CO sts together making
sure that sts do not become twisted on
needle.

P1 rnd.

K all rnds until entire piece measures 4 (5) in.

HEAD

K45 (55) sts. Turn work and P1 row. Turn work and BO 45 (55) sts. Cut yarn, leaving a 10-in. tail.

Attach yarn to RS where work was divided and work the remaining 45 (55) sts in St st until piece measures 2½ in. from divide.

Begin dec, changing to dpns when necessary:

ROW 1 (DEC): (K2tog) 5 times, K to end of row.

ROW 2 (DEC): (P2tog) 5 times, P to end of row.

ROW 3 (DEC): K2tog, K to last 2 sts, K2tog.

ROW 4: P.

ROWS 5–8: Rep Rows 3 and 4 twice.

ROW 9 (DEC): *K2tog; rep from * across row.

ROW 10: P.

Rep Rows 9 and 10 until approx 8 sts remain. Cut yarn, leaving a 10-in. tail. Thread a tapestry needle and pass it through the remaining sts. Pull tightly and—presto!—the head of the blackbird takes shape. With the same tail, sew a seam along the top of the blackbird and secure the remainder of the yarn to the inside of the work.

With the other yarn tail, carefully sew up the width of the blackbird.

SMALL WINGS
(MAKE 2)

With straight needles, CO 3 sts.

ROW 1 (INC): K1f&b, K to last st, K1f&b.

ROW 2: P.

Rep these 2 rows until there are 21 sts on needle.

NEXT ROW (DEC): SSK, K to last 2 sts, K2tog.

NEXT ROW: P.

Rep these 2 rows until 3 sts remain. BO all sts.

LARGE WING
(MAKE 1)

Rep directions for small wings, repeating the 2 inc rows until there are 27 sts. Work dec rows as for small wings.

BEAK
(MAKE 2)

With dpns, CO 8 sts for I-Cord (see p. 114).

ROWS 1–5: Work I-Cord.

ROW 6 (DEC): K2tog, K to last st, K2tog.

ROWS 7 AND 8: Work I-Cord.

Rep Rows 6–8. BO all sts.

knitting tip

Instead of using polyester fill, you can save and use your yarn ends. You don't need too much to stuff this blackbird's head.

FINISHING

Sew large wing onto center seam of back of bird. Sew small wings on each side of center seam on top of large wings.

Attach beaks, letting the beak remain open.

With Firecracker, create 2 French Knots (see p. 113) on either side of head for eyes.

With Firecracker and using Duplicate Stitch (see p. 113), create small decorative Vs on both small wings.

Weave in all loose ends.

Stuff a small amount of polyester filling into head of bird to help keep this beastly blackbird's head held high.

what a Hoot
OWL HAT

Whooooo's wearing the cutest hat around?
This wise and noble owl is a great addition to any
little goblin's Halloween outfit.

SIZING

Small (16-in. circumference)
Large (18-in. to 20-in. circumference)
Figures for larger size are given below in
    parentheses. Where only one set of figures
    appears, the directions apply to both sizes.

YARN

DK weight/light worsted weight yarn
The hat shown is made with Plymouth Yarn
    DK Merino Superwash: 100% fine superwash
    merino wool, 1.75 oz. (50 g)/130 yd. (119 m).

YARDAGE

60 (80) yd. DK Merino Superwash #1020
    Butter
40 (50) yd. DK Merino Superwash #1000 White
20 yd. DK Merino Superwash #1118 Dark Grey
10 yd. DK Merino Superwash #1050 Black
6 yd. DK Merino Superwash #1125 Brown Bear
5 yd. DK Merino Superwash #1108 Sunshine

MATERIALS

16-in. U.S. size 5 circular needle
One pair U.S. size 5 straight needles
Four U.S. size 5 double-pointed needles
Stitch marker
Tapestry needle

GAUGE

22 sts = 4 in.

SEED STITCH

RND 1: *K1, P1: rep from * to end of rnd.
ALL OTHER RNDS: K the P sts and P the K sts.

DIRECTIONS FOR HAT

HAT BASE

With circ needle and White, CO 80 (100)
    sts. Place a st marker on right needle and,
    beginning Rnd 1, join CO sts together making
    sure that sts do not become twisted on
    needle.
P1 rnd.

NEXT RND: Work Loop Stitch (see p. 114) for entire rnd.

K1 rnd.

Cut White and attach Butter. Work in St st until entire piece measures 3 in. from cast-on edge.

NEXT RND (DEC): *K8, K2tog; rep from * to end of rnd.

K5 rnds.

NEXT RND (DEC): *K7, K2tog; rep from * to end of rnd.

K5 rnds.

NEXT RND (DEC): *K6, K2tog; rep from * to end of rnd.

K1 rnd.

RIDGE RND: P.

K8 (10) rnds.

knitting tip

Metal is better! Always use a sharp metal tapestry needle to easily create duplicate stitches, attach embellishments, and weave in your ends.

PEAK DECREASE ROUNDS

NOTE: Place sts on dpns when necessary.

DEC RND: *K4, K2tog; rep from * to end of rnd.

DEC RND: *K3, K2tog; rep from * to end of rnd.

DEC RND: *K2, K2tog; rep from * to end of rnd.

DEC RND: *K1, K2tog; rep from * to end of rnd.

Cut yarn, leaving a 6-in. tail. Thread tapestry needle and pass yarn through remaining sts. Pull tightly. Bring yarn to WS of piece and secure.

EYES

With Sunshine and tapestry needle, and using photo for placement, create 2 circles using Duplicate Stitch (see p. 113). With Black and tapestry needle, sew small running sts to outline the circles. With Black, create a large French Knot (see p. 113) in the center of each eye.

NOSE

With Black and dpns, CO 5 sts. Work I-Cord (see p. 114) for 4 rows.

NEXT ROW: K2tog, K1, K2tog.

Work I-Cord for 10 rows.

K all sts. DO NOT TURN WORK.

Cut yarn, leaving a 3-in. tail. Thread tapestry needle and pass through sts on needle. Work needle through the entire cord until you have both the CO tail and the working tail on the same end of cord. With tapestry needle and yarn tails, sew I-Cord nose to center of owl's face.

EARS

(MAKE 2)

With Dark Grey and straight needles, CO 15 sts, leaving a 6-in. tail for seaming.

Work Seed st for 2 rows.

DEC ROW: SSK, work Seed st to last 2 sts, K2tog.

Work Dec Row every other row until 3 sts remain.

NEXT ROW: SSK, K1.

BO all sts.

Fold each ear triangle at base and, using the tail, sew the CO edge together to create a small cone shape. Using photograph for placement, sew each ear onto owl's face.

FINISHING

With Sand and straight needles, CO 100 (120) sts.

ROW 1: Work Loop Stitch (see p. 114) across row.

BO all sts kwise.

With a tapestry needle and Butter, sew face fur around owl's face using photograph for placement.

With tapestry needle and Brown Bear, use Duplicate Stitch (see p. 113) to create small fur details around back and front of owl.

stinging
BUMBLEBEE
BEANIE AND MITTENS

Buzz, buzz, buzz! This bumblebee will keep any head warm with no stinging involved, while the mittens will keep small hands cozy.

Stinging Bumblebee Beanie

SIZING

Small (18-in. circumference)

Large (21-in. circumference)

Figures for larger size are given below in parentheses. Where only one set of figures appears, the directions apply to both sizes.

YARN

Worsted weight, single-ply yarn

The beanie shown is made with Classic Elite MinnowMerino: 100% extra-fine superwash merino, 1.75 oz. (50 g)/77 yd. (70 m).

YARDAGE

50 (70) yd. MinnowMerino #4750 Goldie

50 yd. MinnowMerino #4701 Snow White

30 (40) yd. MinnowMerino #4713 Jet Black

MATERIALS

16-in. U.S. size 8 circular needle

One pair U.S. size 8 straight needles

Four U.S. size 8 double-pointed needles

Tapestry needle

Stitch marker

Small amount of polyester filling

GAUGE

18 sts = 4 in.

SEED STITCH

RND 1: *K1, P1; rep from * to end of rnd.

ALL OTHER RNDS: K the P sts and P the K sts.

DIRECTIONS FOR BEANIE

HAT BASE

With circ needle and Goldie, CO 76 (84) sts. Place a st marker on right needle and, beginning Rnd 1, join CO sts together making sure that sts do not become twisted on needle.

P1 rnd.

Drop Goldie and attach Jet Black.

RND 1: With Jet Black, *K1, sl 1 wyib; rep from * to end of rnd.

RND 2: *P1, sl 1 wyib; rep from * to end of rnd.

RND 3: Drop Jet Black and K entire rnd with Goldie.

RND 4: With Goldie, P entire rnd.*

Rep Rnds 1–4 once.

Cut Jet Black and, with Goldie, K all rnds until entire piece measures 4 in.

CROWN

K2tog all rounds, placing sts on dpns when necessary, until approx 6 sts remain. Cut yarn, leaving a 6-in. tail. Thread a tapestry needle and pass it through the remaining sts on the needle, pull tightly, and secure.

STRIPES

With Jet Black and using Duplicate Stitch (see p. 113), create the bee's stripes, placing them about 10 sts apart for a total of 8 stripes.

WINGS
(MAKE 4)

With Snow White and straight needles, CO 6 sts. Working in Seed st, inc 1 st (K1f&b) at the beginning and end of every row until there are 20 sts. Work 4 rows in Seed st. Dec (K2tog) every other row until 6 sts remain. BO all sts.

EYES
(MAKE 2)

With Snow White and straight needles, CO 6 sts. Working in Seed st, work approx 8 rows or until you have created a square. Cut yarn, leaving a 6-in. tail. Thread a tapestry needle and pass it through the sts on the needle, then sew a running st along the other 3 sides of the square. Pull tightly until you have created a ball, leaving the yarn tail for sewing later. Thread a tapestry needle with Jet Black and create a French Knot (see p. 113) in the middle of the eye.

ANTENNA EYEBROWS
(MAKE 2)

With Jet Black, CO 3 sts. Create an I-Cord (see p. 114) 3 in. to 4 in. long. Cut yarn, leaving a 3-in. tail. Thread a tapestry needle and pass it through the sts on the needle and then down the center of the I-Cord. Pull the tail slightly to make a squiggle effect for each eyebrow.

FINISHING

Sew 2 wings together, leaving a small side opening. Stuff wings with polyester filling. Sew up final seam. Rep for second wing. Attach wings to crown of hat along seamline.

With tails of eyes, sew eyes onto hat.

With tails of I-Cord, sew antenna eyebrows above eyes.

With Jet Black and a tapestry needle, create a smile on the bee with a small running st.

Weave in all loose ends on wrong side.

Your beasty bumblebee is ready to buzz!

knitting tip

Don't be shy about your color choices. Experiment to make this hat into any fuzzy little insect.

⁎ knitting tip

Go long! If desired, knit the cuff a little longer so you can double it up for a more secure fit.

Stinging Bumblebee Mittens

SIZING
One size (1–2 years)

YARN
Worsted weight, single-ply yarn

The mittens shown are made with Classic Elite MinnowMerino: 100% extra-fine superwash merino, 1.75 oz. (50 g)/77 yd. (70 m).

YARDAGE
40 yd. MinnowMerino #4750 Goldie

30 yd. MinnowMerino #4701 Snow White

15 yd. MinnowMerino #4713 Jet Black

MATERIALS
One pair U.S. size 8 straight needles

Tapestry needle

Stitch marker

Stitch holders

GAUGE
18 sts = 4 in.

SEED STITCH
ROW 1: *K1, P1; rep from * to end of row.

ALL OTHER ROWS: K the P sts and P the K sts.

DIRECTIONS FOR MITTENS

CUFF

With Goldie, CO 32 sts. Work in K2, P2 ribbing for 1 in.

Drop Goldie and attach Jet Black. K1 row. P1 row.

Drop Jet Black and pick up Goldie. K1 row. P1 row.

THUMB

ROW 1 (INC): K14, place marker, K1f&b, K1, K1f&b, place marker, K15. There are now 5 thumb sts between markers.

P1 row.

Drop Goldie and pick up Jet Black.

ROW 2 (INC): With Jet Black, K to marker, sl marker, K1f&b, K3, K1f&b, sl marker, K to end. There are now 7 thumb sts between markers.

K1 row.

Drop Jet Black and pick up Goldie.

ROW 3 (INC): K to marker, sl marker, K1f&b, K5, K1f&b, sl marker, K to end. There are now 9 thumb sts between markers.

P1 row.

ROW 4 (INC): K to marker, sl marker, K1f&b, K7, K1f&b, sl marker, K to end. There are now 11 thumb sts between markers.

P1 row.

DIVIDING ROW: (RS) K to marker and place these 14 sts on a holder.

Remove marker, K11 sts for thumb, remove second marker. Place remaining 14 sts on holder.

Work in St st for 4 rows.

Drop Goldie and pick up Jet Black. K2 rows.

Cut Jet Black and pick up Goldie. K2 rows.

DECREASE ROWS

ROW 1 (DEC): *K1, K2tog; rep from * across row.

P1 row.

ROW 2 (DEC): *K2tog; rep from * across row.

Cut yarn, leaving a 6-in. tail. Thread a tapestry needle and draw end through remaining sts. Pull tightly through all sts. Fasten securely.

BODY

Sl all sts from holder back onto needle. With Jet Black, K entire row.

NEXT ROW: P.

Drop Jet Black and attach Goldie. Work even in St st, working Jet Black row every 4th row, until you have completed 4 Jet Black rows. Cut Jet Black.

ROW 1 (DEC): *K2, K2tog; rep from * across row.

ROW 2: P.

ROW 3 (DEC): *K1, K2tog; rep from * across row.

ROW 4: P.

ROW 5 (DEC): *K2tog; rep from * across row.

WINGS (MAKE 4)

Follow directions for beanie wings (see p. 98), casting on 4 sts, inc to 10 sts, and dec until 4 sts remain.

EYES (MAKE 2)

Follow directions for beanie eyes (see p. 98), casting on 4 sts and working 4 rows.

FINISHING

Cut yarn, leaving an 8-in. tail. Thread a tapestry needle and draw through all sts on needle. Fasten securely.

Using a tapestry needle and a small running st, carefully sew up seams on each mitten, being careful to line up each stripe. Using a small Whip Stitch (see p. 114), carefully sew up thumb seam.

With tails of eyes, sew eyes onto each side of center mitten seam.

With Jet Black and a tapestry needle, create a small smile on the bee immediately below the tip of the mitten.

Weave in all loose ends on wrong side.

Bright
BUTTERFLY
CAP AND SCARF

Surprise! It's an enormous butterfly to welcome spring. The matching cotton scarf has two pockets on each end to hide special spring goodies.

Bright Butterfly Cap

SIZING

Small (16-in. circumference)

Large (20-in. circumference)

Figures for larger size are given below in parentheses. Where only one set of figures appears, the directions apply to both sizes.

YARN

DK weight smooth yarn

The hat shown is made with Westminster Fibers S.R. Kertzer Super 10 Cotton: 100% mercerized cotton, 4.4 oz. (125 g)/250 yd. (229 m).

YARDAGE

80 (100) yd. Super 10 Cotton #3533 Daffodil

40 (50) yd. Super 10 Cotton #0004 White

20 yd. Super 10 Cotton #3062 Turquoise

20 yd. Super 10 Cotton #5701 Basil

10 yd. Super 10 Cotton #3456 Hot Pink

10 yd. Super 10 Cotton #0001 Black

MATERIALS

16-in. U.S. size 4 circular needle

One pair U.S. size 4 straight needles

Four U.S. size 4 double-pointed needles

Stitch marker

Tapestry needle

Small amount of polyester filling

GAUGE

22 sts = 4 in.

SEED STITCH

RND 1: *K1, P1: rep from * to end of rnd.

ALL OTHER RNDS: K the P sts and P the K sts.

DIRECTIONS FOR CAP

CAP BASE

With Daffodil and circ needle, CO 80 (90) sts. Place a st marker on right needle and, beginning Rnd 1, join CO sts together making sure that sts do not become twisted on needle.

P1 rnd.

Work in Seed st for 4 in.

RIDGE ROUNDS

With Daffodil, K1 rnd. P1 rnd.

Cut Daffodil and attach White. Work 12 (15) rows in St st.

DECREASE FOR CROWN

RND 1 (DEC): *K8, K2tog; rep from * to end of rnd.

RND 2 (DEC): *K7, K2tog; rep from * to end of rnd.

Continue with established dec pattern, working 1 less st between dec and placing sts on dpns when necessary, until 4–6 sts remain. Cut yarn, leaving a 6-in. tail. Thread tail through tapestry needle, run needle through remaining sts on needle, and secure tail to WS of work.

WELT

Thread tapestry needle with Daffodil. Pinch the hat at the Ridge Rnd and create a Welt (see p. 114) by sewing together the top and bottom pieces using even running sts.

BUTTERFLY

(MAKE 1 WITH BASIL AND 1 WITH TURQUOISE)

With Basil/Turquoise and straight needles, CO 35 sts.

ROW 1 (AND ALL ODD ROWS): Work in Seed st.

ROW 2 (AND ALL EVEN ROWS; DEC): SSK, K to last 2 sts, K2tog.

Rep Rows 1 and 2 until 19 sts remain. Drop Basil/Turquoise and attach Black.

K4 rows in Garter st.

Cut Black and pick up Basil/Turquoise.

K1 row.

ROW 1 (AND ALL ODD ROWS): Work in Seed st.

ROW 2 (AND ALL EVEN ROWS; INC): K1f&b, K to last st, K1f&b.

Rep Rows 1 and 2 until there are 35 sts. BO all sts.

ANTENNAE
(MAKE 2)

With Black and dpn, CO 4 sts. Work I-Cord (see p. 114) for 3 in. Cut yarn, leaving a 6-in. tail. Thread a tapestry needle and pass needle through remaining 4 sts, then pass through center of I-Cord so that both CO and BO tails are at one end.

FINISHING

With Turquoise, create French Knots (see p. 113) around edges of Basil butterfly. With Hot Pink, create French Knots around edges of Turquoise butterfly. Using a Blanket Stitch (see p. 112) or Whip Stitch (see p. 114), sew Basil and Turquoise butterflies together with WS facing. Before closing up last seam, stuff butterfly with a small amount of polyester filling, if desired, to create a 3-D effect.

Attach each antenna to center edge of butterfly and carefully thread tails through center of Black rows up and down to create a "pinch" in the middle of the butterfly.

Using the tapestry needle, bring the antenna yarn tails to the WS of the peak of the hat and secure tightly. This will help the butterfly sit up straight on top of the hat.

Sew the bottom of the wings to the hat, letting the bottom of the butterfly sit along the peak of the hat so that the butterfly looks like it is about to take off. Or simply let the wings lie flat as if it has just landed on top!

knitting tip

Don't limit your colorways to the hues seen here. Experiment with any bright, spring yarn colors to give your butterfly its own unique look.

Bright Butterfly Scarf

SIZING
One size

YARN
DK weight smooth yarn

The scarf shown is made with Westminster Fibers S.R. Kertzer Super 10 Cotton: 100% mercerized cotton, 4.4 oz. (125 g)/ 250 yd. (229 m).

YARDAGE
110 yd. Super 10 Cotton #3533 Daffodil
10 yd. Super 10 Cotton #3062 Turquoise
10 yd. Super 10 Cotton #3456 Hot Pink
10 yd. Super 10 Cotton #5701 Basil
10 yd. Super 10 Cotton #0001 Black
10 yd. Super 10 Cotton #3402 Tangerine

MATERIALS
One pair U.S. size 4 straight needles
Two U.S. size 4 double-pointed needles
Tapestry needle

GAUGE
22 sts = 4 in.

SEED STITCH
RND 1: *K1, P1: rep from * to end of rnd.
ALL OTHER RNDS: K the P sts and P the K sts.

DIRECTIONS FOR SCARF

SCARF BODY

With Daffodil, CO 40 sts. Work Seed st for 4 in.

ROW 1 (DEC): SSK, K to last 2 sts, K2tog.

ROW 2: Work even in Seed st.

Rep these 2 rows until there are 20 sts.

Continue in Seed st until entire work measures 34 in.

ROW 1 (INC): K1f&b, K to last st, K1f&b.

ROW 2: Work even in Seed st.

Rep these 2 rows until there are 40 sts. BO all sts.

BUTTERFLY

(MAKE 2 WITH TURQUOISE AND 2 WITH HOT PINK)

With Turquoise/Hot Pink, CO 15 sts. Working in Seed st, dec 1 st at each end every other row until you have 9 sts on needle.

Drop Turquoise/Hot Pink and attach Black. K2 rows.

Cut Black and pick up Turquoise/Hot Pink.

Inc 1 st at each end every other row until there are 15 sts. BO all sts.

ANTENNAE

(MAKE 2)

With Black and dpn, CO 2 sts. Work I-Cord (see p. 114) for 2 in. Cut yarn, leaving a 6-in. tail. Thread a tapestry needle and pass needle through 4 sts on needle, then pass through center of I-Cord so that both CO and BO tails are at one end.

FINISHING

With Basil, create French Knots (see p. 113) on one of the Turquoise butterflies. With Tangerine, create Duplicate Stitch (see p. 113) patterns on same Turquoise butterfly. With Tangerine, create French Knots on one of the Hot Pink butterflies. With Turquoise, create Duplicate Stitch patterns on same Hot Pink butterfly.

With Tangerine and tapestry needle, sew 2 Turquoise butterflies together with WS facing using Whip Stitch (see p. 114) or Blanket Stitch (see p. 112). Rep, sewing the Hot Pink butterflies together with Basil.

Attach each antenna to center edge of butterfly and carefully thread tails through center of Black rows up and down to create a "pinch" in the middle of the butterfly.

Using the tapestry needle, bring the antenna yarn tails to the WS and secure tightly.

With Black and tapestry needle, attach each butterfly to scarf in the middle, with antennae pointing up so that they can fly around freely on the scarf.

With Daffodil and tapestry needle, fold the ends of each end of scarf toward the center on the back of the scarf and sew closed. Sew the bottom of each end to create a small pocket.

APPENDIX

Standard
YARN WEIGHTS

NUMBERED BALL	DESCRIPTION	STS/4 IN.	NEEDLE SIZE
1 SUPER FINE	Sock, baby, fingering	27–32	2.25–3.25 mm (U.S. 1–3)
2 FINE	Sport, baby	23–26	3.25–3.75 mm (U.S. 3–5)
3 LIGHT	DK, light worsted	21–24	3.75–4.5 mm (U.S. 5–7)
4 MEDIUM	Worsted, afghan, Aran	16–20	4.5–5.5 mm (U.S. 7–9)
5 BULKY	Chunky, craft, rug	12–15	5.5–8 mm (U.S. 9–11)
6 SUPER BULKY	Bulky, roving	6–11	8 mm and larger (U.S. 11 and larger)

Knitting
NEEDLE SIZES

MILLIMETER RANGE	U.S. SIZE RANGE
2.25 mm	1
2.75 mm	2
3.25 mm	3
3.5 mm	4
3.75 mm	5
4 mm	6
4.5 mm	7
5 mm	8
5.5 mm	9
6 mm	10
6.5 mm	10½
8 mm	11
9 mm	13
10 mm	15
12.75 mm	17
15 mm	19
19 mm	35
25 mm	50

Special
STITCHES

Here are the stitches I use to give my beasties a little something extra special. Read through the instructions and step-by-step illustrations before you start knitting, and you'll have no problem with any of the fun touches that make each beasty unique.

BLANKET STITCH

Thread a tapestry needle with desired color yarn. Bring the needle up from the WS of the work to the RS of the work, about ¼ in. in from the edge. Bring the needle down from the top about ¼ in. over from where the thread first came up and about ⅓ in. from the edge. To complete the first st, bring your needle up from the back and through the loop of the thread. This should create a straight line down on the edge.

BOBBLE

With desired color yarn, K1, P1, K1 in the next st to make 3 sts from 1. Turn and K3. Turn and K3, then lift the second and third sts over the first st on the right needle.

CABLE CAST-ON

Insert right needle between first 2 sts on left needle. Wrap yarn as if to knit. Draw yarn through to complete st and slip this new st onto left needle.

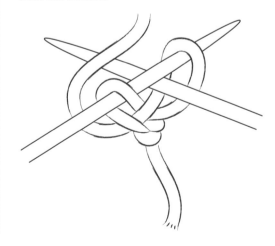

DUPLICATE STITCH

Thread a tapestry needle with the desired color yarn. Bring the needle through from the WS of the work to the base of the knit st you wish to cover with a duplicate st on the front side. Insert the needle directly under the base of the knit st that lies above the st you wish to cover. Bring the needle down and insert it at the base of the same knit st. Bring the tip of the needle out at the base of the next st you wish to cover and repeat this process until you have covered all the desired sts in the design.

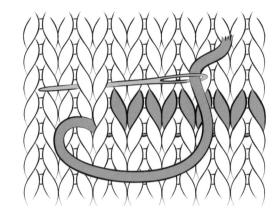

FRENCH KNOT

Thread a tapestry needle with yarn and bring it from the WS of the work to the RS at the point where you wish to place the French Knot. Holding the yarn down with your left thumb, wind the yarn 3 times (for a small knot) or 4 to 6 times (for a large knot) around the needle. Still holding the yarn firmly, twist the needle back to the starting point and insert it close to where the yarn first emerged. Still holding the yarn down with your left thumb, slowly pull the yarn through to the WS to create a French Knot. Secure each knot on WS.

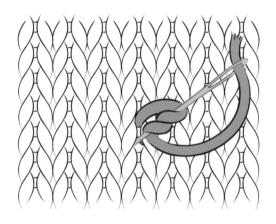

2

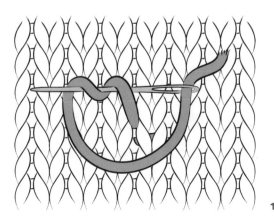

1

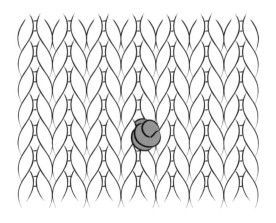

3

I-CORD

With 2 dpns, work I-Cord as follows: Cast on 3 to 6 sts. K sts. *Do not turn work. Slide sts to other end of needle, pull the yarn around the back, and K the sts as usual. Repeat from * for desired length of cord.

LOOP STITCH

K into st, but do not drop the st from the needle. Bring the working yarn to the front of the work. Place your left thumb on the working yarn, and wrap the yarn around and over the top of your thumb, then back between the 2 needles. Keeping the yarn wrapped around your thumb, K into the same st again. You have now created a second st with the loop still on your thumb.

Drop both sts from left needle. You now have 2 new sts and a loop on the right needle. Insert the left needle into the front of the 2 sts on the right needle and K them together.

THREE-NEEDLE BIND-OFF

With right sides of work facing each other, hold needles parallel in your left hand, with the same number of sts on each needle. Hold the third needle in your right hand. *Insert third needle knitwise into both the first st on the needle closest to you and the first st of the back needle. K those 2 sts together. That st is now on the right needle.* Repeat from * to *. Using the tip of one of the needles in your left hand, pass the first st worked over the second st to bind off. Repeat across the row.

WELT

Create a small welt by passing the needle over and under the pieces of knitting that you have "pinched" together, for example, at the side and crown of the hat. Weave both pieces (the side and crown) together using evenly spaced running sts that are approx 1/4 in. from the crown edge. Sewing the 2 pieces together in this way will create a slight thickening or "welt" along the edge of the crown.

WHIP STITCH

Thread a tapestry needle with desired color yarn. Bring the yarn up from the WS of work, leaving a 6-in. tail for weaving in later.

Bring the needle down about 1/8 in. from where you brought the needle up, creating a diagonal st.

Now bring the needle up about 1/8 in. from previous st. Continue stitching, spacing the sts equally and making them all the same length. Be careful not to pull the sts too tightly.

Knitting
ABBREVIATIONS

APPROX: approximately

BEG: beginning

BO: bind off

CIRC: circular

CO: cast on

CONT: continue

DEC: decrease/decreases/decreasing

DPN(S): double-pointed needle(s)

INC: increase/increases/increasing

K: knit

K1F&B: knit in the front and in the back of the same stitch

K2TOG: knit 2 stitches together

KW: knitwise

MB: make bobble

P: purl

PSSO: pass slipped stitch over

PW: purlwise

REM: remaining

REP: repeat

RND: round

RS: right side

SL: slip

ST(S): stitch(es)

ST ST: stockinette stitch

TOG: together

WS: wrong side

WYIB: with yarn in back of work

WYIF: with yarn in front of work

YD: yard(s)

YO: yarn over

Metric
CONVERSION CHART

One inch equals approximately 2.54 centimeters. To convert inches to centimeters, multiply the figure in inches by 2.54 and round off to the nearest half centimeter, or use the chart below, whose figures are rounded off (1 centimeter equals 10 millimeters).

$\frac{1}{8}$ in.	3 mm		9 in.	23 cm
$\frac{1}{4}$ in.	6 mm		10 in.	25.5 cm
$\frac{3}{8}$ in.	1 cm		12 in.	30.5 cm
$\frac{1}{2}$ in.	1.3 cm		14 in.	35.5 cm
$\frac{5}{8}$ in.	1.5 cm		15 in.	38 cm
$\frac{3}{4}$ in.	2 cm		16 in.	40.5 cm
$\frac{7}{8}$ in.	2.2 cm		18 in.	45.5 cm
1 in.	2.5 cm		20 in.	51 cm
2 in.	5 cm		21 in.	53.5 cm
3 in.	7.5 cm		22 in.	56 cm
4 in.	10 cm		24 in.	61 cm
5 in.	12.5 cm		25 in.	63.5 cm
6 in.	15 cm		36 in.	92 cm
7 in.	18 cm		45 in.	114.5 cm
8 in.	20.5 cm		60 in.	152 cm

RESOURCES

DEBBY WARE
www.debbyware.com
www.etsy.com/shop/debbyware

CLASSIC ELITE YARN
16 Esquire Road
North Billerica, MA 01862
www.classiceliteyarns.com

LION BRAND YARNS
34 West 15th Street
New York, NY 10011
www.lionbrand.com

**PLYMOUTH YARN
COMPANY, INC.**
500 Lafayette Street
Bristol, PA 19007
www.plymouthyarn.com

WESTMINSTER FIBERS
(distributor for S.R. Kertzer)
165 Ledge Street
Nashua, NH 03060
www.westminsterfibers.com

INDEX

ABOUT THE AUTHOR

Debby Ware discovered knitting as a child, when her mother taught her the basics, and she has loved it ever since. After graduating from the School of Visual Arts in New York City, she worked for various freelance designers knitting swatches and sample sweaters. She also loved to make one-of-a-kind sweaters for her family and friends.

After owning two successful housewares shops on Martha's Vineyard, Massachusetts, Debby eventually began her pattern and knitting kit business. She now sells her patterns and kits to knitting shops all over the country and online at www.debbyware.com. She lives on Martha's Vineyard with her husband, Will, Buster the Cat, and Maddie the Dog.

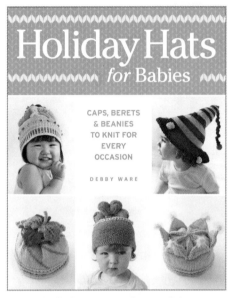